The First Christians

MARIGOLD HUNT

The First Christians
The Acts of the Apostles for Children

SOPHIA INSTITUTE PRESS®
Manchester, New Hampshire

The First Christians was originally published as *The First Catholics* by Sheed and Ward (New York, 1939). This 2004 edition by Sophia Institute Press® contains new illustrations and minor editorial revisions to the original text.

Copyright © 2004 Sophia Institute Press®
All rights reserved
Jacket design and illustrations
by Theodore Schluenderfritz

No part of this book may be reproduced, stored in a retrieval system, or transmitted in any form, or by any means, electronic, mechanical, photocopying, or otherwise, without the prior written permission of the publisher, except by a reviewer, who may quote brief passages in a review.

Sophia Institute Press®
Box 5284, Manchester, NH 03108
1-800-888-9344
www.sophiainstitute.com

Nihil obstat:
Rt. Rev. Edward G. Murray
Diocesan Censor

Imprimatur:
Richard J. Cushing
Archbishop of Boston
August 12, 1953

Library of Congress Cataloging-in-Publication Data

Hunt, Marigold.
 The first Christians : the Acts of the Apostles for children / Marigold Hunt.
     p. cm.
 Rev. ed. of: The first Catholics.
  ISBN: 978-1-62282-909-5
 1. Bible stories, English—N.T. Acts. 2. Catholic Church—Doctrines—Juvenile literature. [1. Bible stories, English—N.T. Acts. 2. Catholic Church—Doctrines.] I. Hunt, Marigold. First Catholics. II. Title.
BS2628.H85 2003
226.6'09505—dc22   2003028059

Contents

Introduction 3

1. How Our Church Began 15
2. The First Adventurers 27
3. The First Persecution 37
4. Saul 51
5. Peter's Vision 59
6. Saul's First Great Journey 75
7. The Council of Jerusalem 89
8. The Second Great Journey Begins 99
9. Paul Goes On Alone 111
10. The Riot in Ephesus 123
11. Paul's Arrest in Jerusalem 135
12. Paul Goes to Rome 155
    Biographical Note 167

The First Christians

Introduction

The Acts of the Apostles is a true story, and an exciting one — nobody ever had more adventures or faced more dangers than the first Christians. St. Luke wrote the Acts after he had written his Gospel, as a continuation of the same story, a second volume.

In his Gospel, St. Luke had told of how our Lord founded His kingdom in spite of everything His enemies could do to prevent it and how hard they had tried — from the time when Herod had killed all of the boy babies in Bethlehem because he thought that was the way to be sure of killing our infant Lord, to the time when the leaders of our Lord's own people turned Him over to the Romans to be crucified. That seemed, at the time, like the end of everything, but of course it wasn't: His death, as we all know, was the very thing that opened the gates of Heaven to us all — He was really triumphing completely over His enemies just when He seemed to have failed.

St. Luke had written about all that. He told about how our Lord had said that His followers could expect just the same kind of treatment that He had received,

The First Christians

and just as it had not prevented Him from founding His Kingdom, so it would not prevent them from spreading it over the world. Our Lord had told the Apostles that they would be brought before governors and kings to be tried as enemies for doing His work, and that they must expect to be imprisoned and beaten and killed and that, just the same, the work would go on and nothing could stop it.

St. Luke could see it all happening already, just as our Lord had said it would, and he thought, "I must write about this, too." So he did, and the Acts of the Apostles is the book he wrote.

Suppose he had gone to sleep just after he finished writing it, and had slept and slept and only woken up again today. He would have had a lot of surprises, wouldn't he? But he would find that though our Lord's Kingdom has spread amazingly, its members are still being treated very much as the first Christians were. You can hardly pick up a newspaper without seeing something about Catholic bishops and priests being put on trial and jailed, or beaten and killed for going on with the work of spreading our Lord's Kingdom. The story of the Church is all one story: we won't find the first chapters surprising and St. Luke wouldn't find our chapter surprising, and this is really rather odd when you remember how much everything else has changed since those days. It's just because everything has changed so much that I have written this book.

There are all sorts of things that St. Luke takes for granted we will understand, because when he wrote anybody would have understood them, but that seem thoroughly puzzling to us. Some are small things easily

Introduction

explained, like calling nine o'clock in the morning the "third hour of the day," and some are large things, not so easy to explain, such as what being told to go and convert the whole world meant to the Apostles. We are used to thinking of the world as a round ball with the north pole at the top and the south pole at the bottom and all the continents and seas neatly arranged in between. But when St. Luke wrote no one thought of the world in the least like that.

They thought of Rome as the center of it, and the farthest away places that the Romans had been to as the edges of it — anyway as the edges of anything that mattered. Now the Romans had been a very long way — to Spain and England, to Germany and Africa and far over toward China, but that leaves quite a lot of world unaccounted for, doesn't it? There were two whole continents they didn't know existed and much more of Europe and Asia and Africa than they guessed.

So when the Apostles were told to go and convert the "whole world" they had no idea what a large job God was giving them.

In fact they really thought that if they worked very hard, they might get it done in their own lifetimes. If they had been told that nearly two thousand years later it still wouldn't be finished, I don't know what they would have thought! God's plans have a way of being larger than we suppose and He doesn't usually tell us more about them than we need to know to do our part in them properly.

Of course if we had all worked as hard at converting the world as the Apostles did, it would certainly be done by now: they had got an astonishing amount done

The First Christians

by the time they were killed. Thomas had preached as far away as India to the east, and James had been all the way to Spain.

One thing that helped them was that the Romans were very good at making roads and all the world they had reached was linked up with good wide roads on which soldiers could march and horses be ridden and driven. If you have ever gone for a walk in the country where there was no road and had to scramble through thick woods and wade through streams and climb hills, you will understand what a terrific difference it makes in the time it takes to get anywhere whether you have a road to travel on or not.

Nothing is more fun than walking across country away from roads, I know, but if you are trying to reach a place one hundred miles away, it is no fun at all. Another thing about the Romans that helped the Apostles was that they were good at making laws, and seeing that they were kept, and that made the world a safer place than it had been. Not that it was so very safe — there were plenty of robbers and bandits about, and no one dared go on a long journey alone. But still it was much better than it had been.

Introduction

And if you were accused of a crime the Romans would at least hear what you had to say about it before allowing you to be punished, and if you were punished it was done according to the law and not just according to how your judge happened to be feeling at the time.

In those days the thing to be was a Roman citizen. That didn't mean somebody who lived in Rome, as you might suppose, it meant anyone at all, wherever he lived, who counted as just as good as a Roman. If the Romans were pleased with you for being a particularly good soldier or for being very useful to them in some other way, they would make you a Roman citizen as a reward, whatever country you belonged to. Or you could become one by paying a large sum of money, if you were rich enough. Sometimes all the inhabitants of a city were made Roman citizens, and that had happened to the people in Tarsus, St. Paul's city, which is how he happened to be a Roman citizen.

To be a Roman citizen was a great help because it meant that you couldn't be beaten or crucified and you could only be tried by a Roman court, according to Roman law, and if you thought you were not getting a fair trial, you could appeal to Caesar and be sent to Rome to have your case heard there. People who were not Roman citizens were either slaves, or, as people are now, citizens of whatever country they happened to have been born in.

Now one last thing, and then we can really get started. Most of the people you will read about in this book were our Lord's people, the Jews: all the Apostles and their first converts were Jewish, and for some time not only the Romans, but the Christians, too, thought

The First Christians

of a Christian as just a new sort of Jew. And in a way, of course, so we are. Our Lord's Kingdom on earth, the Church we belong to, is the Kingdom that was prophesied in the Old Testament. But now it is for everybody, Jews or not.

It took quite a time, as you will see, for the Jewish Christians to realize that whether you are Jewish or not simply didn't matter any more, and that the special rules and ceremonies God gave to His people under the Old Law no longer counted. It is important to understand that they loved their religion and were very proud of having been given it by God: who wouldn't be?

They had the great Temple in Jerusalem as the center of everything, the only place where sacrifices were offered to God. We don't much like the idea of those sacrifices, of killing lambs or other animals as presents to God, but it seemed perfectly right to them, and so it was. All these things were foreshadowings of our Lord's sacrifice and until the Last Supper and Calvary gave us the Mass, they were the right way to worship God.

There were prayers and singing in the Temple every day, seven times a day, and great crowds there on feast days. But everybody in the country couldn't be in Jerusalem every feast day, let alone every Sabbath day, so in each town and village they had a place to meet for prayers and readings from the Scriptures every week. These places were called synagogues, and the Jews still have them everywhere they are, though they no longer have the Temple in Jerusalem.

The old Jewish religion was full of rules to keep: so many rules that the ordinary idea was that to keep them all was the whole of being good. They needed our Lord

Introduction

to teach them that *why* you do a thing can matter more than what you do.

I mean, if you only go to Mass on Sunday because you hope to meet someone afterwards who will invite you to come and watch television in his house, that wouldn't be being good, would it? And if you stayed away from Mass because you were in quarantine for measles, that wouldn't be wrong. For the first we should need to go to Confession, but the second would leave our souls quite clean. Many of the Jews wouldn't have understood that. They had to learn by degrees and by practicing keeping the rules God had given them. Numbers of these rules were about keeping their bodies clean and were meant to prepare them to understand what an awful thing a dirty soul is and how important it is to keep *that* clean.

For instance, if they touched a dead person or someone with leprosy, they had to wash themselves and wash their clothes and wait until sunset before they were considered clean again. And some animals were never to be eaten because they counted as unclean. One sort were pigs. If you have Jewish friends who keep their rules, you know that they still won't eat pork or bacon.

But if the rules to keep under the Old Law (and I can't begin to tell you how many of them there were) were a nuisance, they had lovely feasts which they enjoyed just as we enjoy Easter and Christmas. The Paschal feast was one of them. It was in remembrance of the way God had brought them out of slavery in Egypt and a foretelling of our Lord's death, only they didn't know that. Everybody had roast lamb and salad and sweet wine for this feast and ate unleavened bread

The First Christians

for a whole week. If you have any Jewish friends you could ask them to tell you about how they keep this feast now and about Chanukah, the Feast of Lights in winter, near Christmas time, and a summer feast that I am sure the children enjoyed most of all.

This was called the Feast of Tabernacles and was in memory of the time when they were on their way to the Holy Land and had no proper houses. They celebrated it by making shelters from the boughs of trees and going and camping out for a week! I wish we could have that one, though for people living in big cities like London or New York it might be a little difficult to arrange. And every month when the new moon was due to appear the priests in the Temple watched for it, and as soon as it was seen, they all blew trumpets. I expect the boys in Jerusalem helped by shouting as loud as they could or blowing trumpets, too!

Now just think: how would we feel if we were told one day that we needn't keep Lent any more nor celebrate Easter; there would be no more Easter eggs and no holiday, and we needn't go to Mass on Sunday, and there would be no Christmas next winter, no crib, and no Christmas trees or stockings hung up. I think we would feel as if the world had turned upside down.

Don't worry, it won't happen, but the way we would feel if it did is rather like the way the Jews who had become Christian felt when they were told that the old rules no longer mattered and the old feasts need no longer be kept.

No wonder the first Christians were slow to understand it. In fact, to begin with they seem to have gone on with all the things they were used to and just added

Introduction

the Mass on as well. This didn't matter a bit — none of these things were wrong, after all — until the question came up of what to do about people who were not Jews becoming Christians. That's where the trouble started.

The Jewish Christians hadn't realized that people who were not Jews could become Christians and that when they became Christians they need not keep any of the old Jewish rules, and this seemed terrible at first. They had believed for so long that they were God's people and the rest of the world were just Gentiles in whom God wasn't interested.

It's true that any Gentile who really wanted to could become a Jew and count as just as good as if he'd been born Jewish so long as he kept all the rules.

But the idea of these awful Gentiles being allowed to become Christians and to be just as good as anyone else without keeping the rules gave them an awful shock.

Under the Old Law, a man came into the Jewish church by having a small operation that was called circumcision, which marked him as belonging to God's Chosen People. It was done for all Jewish boy babies when they were eight days old. But now that Baptism was the way that you became a Christian, circumcision didn't matter any more and this they found almost too hard to understand.

If the Jews who became Christians found it hard to realize all this, what about the Jews who didn't believe the Apostles' preaching? They were outraged! They felt about people who joined the Church rather as we feel about people who leave the Church, that they were throwing away everything God had given them.

The First Christians

So now you see why all through Acts there is trouble over this, not only from the Jews who hadn't joined the Church, but also from some of those who had.

In the end it all got sorted out, of course, but for a long time St. Paul was the only person who realized that it would have to be. He was the first to see that as long as the Jewish converts went on keeping all the rules of the old religion they would be sure to think of themselves as a better sort of Christian than the Gentile converts and that this would mean two grades of Christian, and would never do.

The curious thing is that just as the Jews in those days felt that they were the most important people in the whole world and were quite wrong, so nowadays you will sometimes hear people talk as if the Jews were less important than other people. That is just as silly as the other idea. Everyone is exactly as important as everyone else, and all the people in the world are equally welcome in the kingdom of God, which is His Church on earth. Only if you do happen to be Jewish and to be a Christian, too, it must be especially nice to know that you belong to our Lord's people in that way, as well as belonging to Him in every other way.

So many of the people in this book are saints, and there are so many more that are probably saints, that I thought you would get rather tired of reading "St." in front of all their names, so I have done as St. Luke did and left it out. I don't think the saints will mind in the least — after all, they weren't called saints when they were living.

Chapter One

How Our Church Began
(Acts 1, 2)

Luke ended his Gospel with our Lord's Ascension into Heaven, and he begins this new book by telling about it again, as though he wanted to give us just one more glimpse of our Lord before going on to the story of how the Apostles spread His Kingdom over the world.

For forty days after the first Easter Sunday, he tells us, our Lord stayed on earth, coming to see His Apostles often, and no doubt, His other friends too, and teaching them more about the kingdom of God. At the end of that time He came to share a last meal with them — it was probably breakfast, though no one can be quite certain about it.

While they were eating, our Lord told them that they were to stay in Jerusalem and wait for the fulfillment of His Father's promise.

They very likely said, as I daresay you are saying, "What promise?" For our Lord went on, "You have heard it from my own lips. John's baptism was with water, but there is a baptism with the Holy Spirit which you are to receive, not many days from now." The Apostles had already been baptized both with John the

The First Christians

Baptist's kind of baptism which was not a sacrament, but only a sign that you were sorry for your sins, and also as we are baptized now. But this was to be something new: nothing quite like it had ever happened before or would ever happen again. Sometimes it is called the birthday of the Church and sometimes a special sort of Baptism for the whole Church, or a Confirmation of the whole Church.

The Holy Spirit comes to strengthen us when we are confirmed — "confirmation" means strengthening — and whatever we call it, His coming now was a tremendous strengthening of the whole Church. To be strengthened and steadied, made firm in their Faith, was just what the Apostles needed.

They still didn't understand what the kingdom of God was to be like, they still hoped our Lord was going to reign as ordinary kings do and make His nation the greatest in the world. So they said to Him, "Lord, are you going to restore the Kingdom to Israel now?"

Our Lord didn't say, "Oh, for goodness' sake, don't be so silly!" He just told them that was not really any of their business, and that it was enough for them to know that the Holy Spirit would come to them and give them the strength to be witnesses to Him everywhere — in Jerusalem and Judea and Samaria and beyond there, to the very ends of the earth.

While the Apostles and our Lord were talking they finished breakfast and had walked out from Jerusalem across the valley to the hill opposite, the Mount of Olives. Then they went around the hill a little way to visit Bethany where Martha and Mary and Lazarus lived.

How Our Church Began

Such a lot of things had happened at Bethany: our Lord had been staying with the family there only a few days before He was killed; and it was just a little while before that He had brought Lazarus back to life after he had been dead for four days; and it was from Bethany that our Lord had set out on the day when He was met by the crowds strewing branches of palms and cheering for Him.

Martha and Mary and Lazarus must have been very special friends of His, so He went to say good-bye to them. Luke doesn't say in the Acts that He went to Bethany on His way up the Mount of Olives, but he does say so at the end of his Gospel, so I have put it in here, because it was so nice of our Lord to go and see His friends before He went back to Heaven.

From the top of the Mount of Olives, which is just a little higher than Jerusalem, there is a wonderful view. You can see all across the hills to the Dead Sea on one side, and on the other you see Jerusalem spread out like a map on the side of the hill across the valley. I have been there once, at just about the time of year the Ascension happened, and it was a bright sunny day with little clouds flying over the sky. I thought they probably looked very like the cloud that at last hid our Lord from the Apostles when He went up into the sky, and I stood there looking at them and thinking what a lovely place our Lord had chosen to go back to Heaven from.

A man selling rosary beads came and interrupted me, but the people watching our Lord were only persuaded to stop looking up when two angels came and stood by them and said, "Men of Galilee, why are you

The First Christians

standing here looking up to Heaven? Jesus, whom you have watched going up to Heaven, will return at last in just the same way."

After that, they all went back to Jerusalem, and, as we would say, made a retreat. Our Lady and her friends, the other holy women, and the Apostles and all our Lord's friends gathered together in the big upper room where the Last Supper had been eaten. They prayed a lot and waited quietly and went out as little as they could, except to go to the Temple.

Besides praying together, there was something else that Peter felt ought to be attended to. So one day he stood up and spoke to all of them. He reminded them that Judas had proved a traitor and was now dead, and that this left the number of the Apostles only eleven instead of twelve. "So," he said, "we ought to choose somebody else to take his place, as a witness of the Resurrection."

It had to be a man who had been a disciple of our Lord all through His public life and who had seen Him after He rose from the dead. There were two men there,

How Our Church Began

Matthias and Justus, who seemed as if they would do very well, and no one knew which to choose, so they prayed very hard that God would show them which one He wanted to be the twelfth Apostle, and then they drew lots. We don't know how they did this — perhaps they gave them two pieces of straw to choose from and the one that got the short piece was to be chosen. But however they did it, Matthias won and was counted as the twelfth Apostle after that.

The funny thing is that we never hear any more about Matthias but we do know something more about Justus — he became a bishop and died a martyr.

This first retreat in the upper room lasted for nine days. Then, early in the morning, everyone gathered there heard a noise of a great wind blowing. The sound filled the whole house, and in the wind they saw flames, which came to rest on them and parted into separate tongues.

These flames didn't burn them — they had quite a different effect. You have heard a language called a tongue, haven't you?

The First Christians

Well, one effect of these parted tongues of fire was to make them able to speak in languages they had never learned. And besides that, and more important still, they all suddenly felt very strong and brave and cheerful and ready for anything.

Fire gives us light and warmth, and that's just what the Apostles were given: light to understand all that our Lord had taught them and the warmth of the love of God which made them ready to give their lives to spread His Kingdom over the world.

Our Lord had told them, "When He, the Spirit of Truth, has come, He will lead you into all truth and bring to your minds all that I have taught you." Now it had happened: the Apostles had everything they needed for the work they were to do, so out they all went straight away, and started doing it. Wherever there was room for a crowd in the city they stood and preached about our Lord to whoever would listen.

There were a great many people in Jerusalem who came from other countries: Jews whose homes were abroad and who had come to Jerusalem for the feast day which was held every year in memory of the giving of the Law of the Old Testament to Moses. It was the same day, of course, as we keep Pentecost now. When the Apostles came running out into the streets and began to speak of our Lord, there were plenty of people to listen: it was just the time everyone was starting out for nine o'clock prayers in the Temple. So almost at once each Apostle had a crowd listening to him.

But see how clever the Holy Spirit had been! If they had just spoken their own language, a lot of people would probably have said, "Oh, those people again — I thought that was all over." But when these people from faraway countries heard the Apostles speaking in the languages they were accustomed to hear there, they were so astonished they didn't know what to do. The Apostles, you see, didn't look at all rich and grand and traveled: they looked like just what they were, mostly Galilean fishermen.

Suppose that you went to Rome and heard an old man who didn't look as if he had ever been out of Italy in his life making a speech in just the sort of English you were used to hearing in Ohio. And if you had a friend from the French-speaking part of Canada and he rushed up to you and said, "There's a young man down there, who I'm sure has never been to Canada, but he is speaking in just the sort of French we use in Quebec!" And if a German friend came up then and said, "That's nothing — the same man has just started talking German, and I would swear he had lived all his life in Berlin!" And if the first man changed over to Irish Gaelic just then — well, you see why the crowds in Jerusalem were so surprised and so ready to listen on that first Pentecost Sunday in Jerusalem.

When Luke is telling about the coming of the Holy Spirit, he says that the Apostles began to speak in different languages, but when he is talking of what the crowds who listened to them said, he says everyone heard them speak in the language of his home country.

No one is sure if that means that, whatever language the Apostles spoke, the people listening heard them talking in their own language — as though you spoke English to a Frenchman but he heard what you were saying in French — or if it only means that the Apostles spoke all the languages of the people listening to them. However it was done, it had just the effect God wanted: it made the crowds stop in astonishment and listen.

Of course there were some people about even on the day of Pentecost, who couldn't possibly admit they were impressed. These people just looked very wise and amused and said to each other, "Take no notice, can't you see these men are drunk?"

Peter answered very sensibly. "Why," he said, "it's only nine o'clock in the morning! Whoever heard of men being drunk at that hour." And then he went on to tell them, as all the Apostles were doing, what was really happening, and that Jesus whom they had crucified was God, and that they ought to have believed in Him instead of killing Him.

The sermon he preached to them is in the second chapter of the Acts of the Apostles: it's well worth finding it and reading it — after all, this is the very first sermon by the very first pope.

What he and the other Apostles said impressed the crowds so much that three thousand people were converted that first day. And that was only the beginning.

God gave the Apostles power to work miracles and these miracles and their preaching together brought more and more people into the Church. All of them shared all they had: if they had any possessions of their own they sold them and shared the money.

It was rather as if the whole Church began as one big religious order. For of course sharing everything and not counting your belongings as your own is the way all religious orders live. They don't want to be bothered with such things, but to give all their time to God, and

How Our Church Began

that was just how the first members of the Church felt: why bother with making money and getting possessions when working for God is so much more interesting? So if you want to live like the very first Catholics, just decide to be a monk or a nun!

But, you may remember, there are two kinds of religious orders; we need them both today and must have needed them both quite as much then.

All the things that the Apostles, and the other people who came to help them, were doing to spread the kingdom of God over the world — everything you read about in this book — are the kind of things done now by what are called the Active Orders.

The priests who are missionaries nowadays and the sisters who nurse in hospitals and teach in schools and the brothers who look after orphan boys, and so on, all belong to Active Orders.

The other sort are called Contemplative Orders, and are only for our Lord's very special friends. The people who belong to this kind of Order do even more for us than the Active ones, but we can't see what they are doing, so we often don't think of them at all.

They spend all their time making up for the things the rest of us don't bother about. We don't love God enough to spend much time praying to Him, so they spend their whole lives in prayer; we aren't sorry enough for our sins to do hard penance for them, so they do them for us; and we aren't nearly grateful enough to God for all He does for us, so they thank Him for us, too.

Now who do you think was doing this among the first Christians? Who could it be but our Lady?

The First Christians

I am sure the whole baby Church was as much our Lady's care as her own Baby had been and that for the twelve years or so she continued to live in Jerusalem, she spent nearly all her time between praying at home and praying in the Temple, and that only when the Apostles got to Heaven did they realize how much her prayers had had to do with their wonderful success.

I expect John, our Lord's special friend, understood best, because, you remember, when our Lord was dying He gave our Lady and John to each other to be like mother and son, and I think John was the one of the Apostles who did the most praying and the least preaching, and that is why you hear so little about him in Acts, and why he wrote such a wonderful Gospel.

I think Mary Magdalen and some of the other women who followed our Lord when He was going about preaching, and whom you never hear of again after He went back to Heaven, were this kind of special friend of His, too.

Chapter Two

The First Adventurers

(Acts 3, 4, 5)

We know how our Lord loved the Temple in Jerusalem, and that in addition to praying there, He often walked in its porches while He talked to His friends, and that He used them as good places to teach anyone who would listen about the kingdom of God.

These porches were paved walks against the side of the Temple buildings, open to the air on one side, but with roofs supported by pillars. Most convents and monasteries have a place like that, called a cloister, where people can sit or walk in the air but out of the rain or cold wind. I expect you have seen one.

Now the Apostles went on going to the Temple to pray after our Lord went back to Heaven, and they also used to use the porches as a good place to tell people about Him.

Well, one afternoon as Peter and John were going into the Temple courtyard by the entrance called the Beautiful Gate, they saw a man carried along and set down on the ground beside it. He was carried because he couldn't walk: he was crippled and had no strength in his feet or legs.

The First Christians

For his living he used to sit every day beside the Beautiful Gate and beg from everyone who went through it. He begged from Peter and John as soon as he saw them. Both of them stopped and Peter said, "Look at us."

I suppose the man had given up on them — two poor fishermen wouldn't have looked like good people to beg from — and was asking someone else. But he turned to them as soon as he heard Peter speak and looked at them as hard as ever he could, thinking they must mean to give him something.

Peter said, "I have no silver or gold, but I will give you what I can. In the name of Jesus of Nazareth, get up and walk!"

The crippled man just stared at him in astonishment. But Peter took him by the hand and pulled him to his feet and he found he could stand! He could walk! He could jump! And although he was a middle-aged man, he was so excited that he did jump. He went into the Temple with Peter and John, jumping up and down with excitement and praising God out loud and no wonder. All three of them arrived in Solomon's porch, the man who had been crippled holding onto Peter and John and telling everybody what had happened. Of course people crowded about them, very much astonished, because everybody knew the crippled man: they had seen him so often sitting begging by the Beautiful Gate. And here he was prancing about and saying it was all Peter and John's doing that he was cured.

Peter thought it was time he did a little explaining. "Men of Israel, why are you so surprised?" he said, "Why look at us as if we had made this man walk by our own

The First Adventurers

power? It was God who did it, of course, to honor His Son, Jesus." And he went on to tell them how wrong they had been not to believe in our Lord and how now they ought to be sorry and to show it by joining His followers.

You will find all that Peter said in the third chapter of the Acts of the Apostles: I don't want to give you all of it here, because if I put in everything that is in the real Acts of the Apostles, you may wonder whether you need bother to read it. The sensible thing to do is to read each chapter of Acts before you read what I say, and then read it again afterwards to see if what I said was helpful.

While Peter and John were still telling the crowd that had gathered around our Lord, up came a number of extremely cross people asking what on earth all the noise was about. They were the chief priest, the Temple superintendent and some of the Sadducees.

The Sadducees were people who didn't believe that the dead were to rise again: you may remember that they once had an argument with our Lord about it and came off very badly. Well, naturally they couldn't stand the Apostles, who not only preached that every one of us would rise again on the last day, but also said that our Lord *had* risen already.

All these people considered themselves very important indeed and the Apostles very unimportant, and they were furious at all the fuss over the cured man.

They didn't really at all know what to do about it, but they arrested Peter and John and the cured man and put them all in prison until the next day, so that they could have time to think. That didn't prevent a great

The First Christians

number of the people who had been there from joining the Church: the number of Christians went up to five thousand that very day!

Next morning, Peter and John were brought out to be tried before the High Priest, Annas (before whom our Lord had been brought for trial), and the rulers and elders and lawyers, and everyone else who was important enough to be invited to be there.

Peter and John were asked, "By what power and in whose name have men like you done this?"

As if they hadn't been telling everybody that all along! The Holy Spirit told Peter how to answer their question. "If it is over the kindness done to a crippled man that you are trying us," he said, "listen to me: I have some news for you! You crucified Jesus Christ, the Man

The First Adventurers

God raised up from death, and it is by His power that this man who was crippled is able to stand up before you."

You know, I doubt if those Very Important People ever felt sillier, and they must have been frightened, too. They remembered how they had treated our Lord and how they had insisted on the Romans crucifying Him, and had thought that was the end of His claims, and now the whole thing seemed to be starting again, and in a most embarrassing way.

They could see that Peter and John were just poor fishermen with very little education — they called them "illiterate nobodies" — but they didn't seem to be in the least frightened. And worst of all, here was the man who had been crippled standing up on his feet (and perhaps jumping a little, now and then).

There was no hope of pretending that he wasn't the same man who had never been able to walk before — too many people knew him: they had all seen him begging by the Beautiful Gate.

What were they to do? Plainly, they didn't know, so they sent Peter and John out of the room while they talked it over.

What they decided at last was that, since there was no denying the miracle, the news of it must be stopped from spreading. Could anything have been sillier? They knew perfectly well that the news was all over Jerusalem and everybody was talking about it and trying to find someone who hadn't heard the story so they could tell it again. And all they could think of was to tell Peter and John and the crippled man they must never mention it and never teach people about our Lord!

The First Christians

They threatened them with all the awful things that would happen to them if they disobeyed this order, and I really think Peter and John must have found it difficult not to smile. They answered very sensibly, "Do you really think we ought to listen to you instead of to God?"

The Important People had no answer to that except more threats: they dared not put the Apostles and the crippled man back in prison because they were afraid of one thing that Important People always fear — what people would say. So at last there was nothing for it but to let them go free.

They went back to their friends and all together they rejoiced and praised God for what He had done through them and they prayed for strength and courage to go on teaching confidently in spite of everyone's threats. When they finished praying, the Holy Spirit came to strengthen and encourage them still more, and the house they were in rocked to and fro as a sign of His presence. An odd sign, you may think, but I imagine they were all what people long after used to call "merry in God" — full of gaiety, like people in Heaven — and that the house rocking may have fitted in very well with their mood. Perhaps this sort of gaiety and excitement was one reason some people thought the Apostles were drunk on the day of Pentecost.

As I told you, the people in the new young Church of our Lord were sharing all they had with each other. One of the new converts was called Barnabas, a man you will hear more about. He came from the island of Cyprus where he had an estate, but he sold it and brought the money to the Apostles.

The First Adventurers

There was never any rule that people who joined the Church had to do this, it just seemed a good idea while the Church was getting started that everyone should share and no one be obliged to worry about possessions. But there was one couple, a husband and wife called Ananias and Sapphira, who thought they would like the credit for selling their estate and bringing all the money to the Apostles, but who meant to cheat.

They thought if they brought just some of the money and pretended it was the whole lot, then everyone would think how good they were and there would be a nice little sum left in the bank.

That sin, telling lies to make people think you are better than you are, is called hypocrisy and it always made our Lord very angry. He was not likely to let hypocrites deceive the Apostles. So when Ananias came in with the money, Peter knew at once that it was not the whole price of his estate. "You have cheated God, not man," he said, and at those words Ananias fell down and died.

Luke doesn't say whether Peter knew that was going to happen or not, he just says that some of the young men picked Ananias up and took him out to bury him. When Sapphira came in later, Peter gave her a chance to tell the truth, but she lied, too, and like her husband, died then and there, just as the men who had buried her husband came back.

When the story of what had happened to these two went around everybody who heard it was very much frightened, and I don't wonder.

If you are ever tempted to try to make people think you are better than you are, just remember Ananias and

The First Christians

Sapphira! Not that you are likely to fall down dead, but so you will remember that hypocrisy is one thing our Lord really hates. We don't know, by the way, if Ananias and Sapphira went to hell. They may have been sorry at the last moment after all.

Chapter Three

The First Persecution

(Acts 5 cont., 6, 7, 8)

The Apostles still went on teaching in Solomon's porch in the Temple, and all their converts used to join them there, but people who were not sure about being Christians kept away — they were afraid of the Important People, and also they had heard what happened to Ananias and Sapphira and were frightened in case something of the sort might happen to them.

On the other hand, the news about the way the Apostles cured sick people was getting known everywhere, even far out in the country. So wherever the Apostles went in Jerusalem there were crippled and blind men and people with all kinds of diseases lining the streets, and even Peter's shadow falling on them cured them.

But all this didn't make the High Priest and his friends happy or more willing to listen to what the Apostles taught. Just as the more miracles our Lord worked, the more furious these people were, so it was now. The more cures and wonders they heard of, the more they hated the Apostles. At last they simply couldn't bear it another moment. So they plucked up their courage and had all the Apostles arrested and clapped into prison.

This happened in the evening: it was too late to do any more then, so the Apostles were just left there for the night. Next morning the High Priest summoned his Council and when everything was ready sent to the prison for the Apostles.

That was all very well, but where were they? All the guards were awake and on duty, all the doors that should have been locked were locked — everything was in perfect order, in fact — only the prison was empty!

How they must have searched and blamed each other and nearly gone frantic before one of the guards went back to the Council and reported that he couldn't imagine how it happened, but the prisoners were not to be found.

I think the solemn Council must have got rather red in the face, don't you? But I would like even more to have seen what they looked like when someone came in and said, "By the way, I thought you put those men who preach in the Temple in prison? Well, did you know they are there now, preaching as usual?"

Can you guess what had happened? God didn't want the Apostles to be in prison just then, there was too much for them to do, so He had simply sent an angel to let them out again. The angel told them to go to the Temple and preach as usual, so early in the morning they had gone there and started off.

When the Council had recovered from this piece of news, they sent officers to go and get the Apostles — as politely as possible, because they were afraid of making everyone furious if the officers behaved roughly.

The First Persecution

The Apostles came willingly enough, but I imagine they had difficulty in keeping their faces suitably solemn.

When they arrived, the High Priest said, "We particularly warned you not to preach in this man's name and you do nothing else — you are determined we shall be blamed for his death!"

Peter and the other Apostles answered, "God has more right to be obeyed than men. It was He who raised up Jesus, the man you killed: He is the Prince and Savior who is to bring us repentance and forgiveness of sins. We are witnesses to this, with the Holy Spirit God gives to all who obey Him."

This made the Important People so furious they wanted to put all the Apostles to death there and then. But there was at least one good and sensible man in the Council. He was called Gamaliel, and he asked that the Apostles should be put in another room for a few minutes. When they were gone, he reminded the Council that twice before a man had appeared who had collected a number of followers, and who had been thought someone special. But each time, after his death, his followers had dwindled away.

"If this is another affair of that sort," said Gamaliel, "it will come to nothing, too. But suppose it is God's doing? You had better be careful — you do not want to find yourselves fighting against God!"

As everybody began to calm down, they saw that this was sensible. So they decided to have the Apostles scourged — just to discourage them, I suppose — and then let them go, with another warning about what would happen if they did not stop preaching about our Lord.

The First Christians

After they had been scourged, the Apostles went home full of that sort of happiness that people who do not love our Lord cannot understand at all. They were delighted to have been allowed to suffer something for Him, and they went on preaching Him openly, both in the Temple and in people's houses.

That trouble from the Church's enemies was over for the moment, but now comes the first of all the troubles the Church has had from her own members.

To understand it, you must first understand that in those days nearly everyone spoke some Greek, whatever their own language was, just as in America nearly everyone speaks some English, even if they have only lately come from Europe and their own language is something quite different.

The Apostles' own language, and the language of everyone who grew up in our Lord's country, was Aramaic, which is a kind of Hebrew, but they nearly all spoke some Greek too.

But many of the new converts were Jews from abroad who had Greek for their own language and did not speak Aramaic at all, and this made them feel rather strange and out of things in Jerusalem. Some of these Greek-speaking Jews complained to the Apostles that when food and clothing and so on were given out from the common fund, they didn't get their fair share. The poor widows among them, they said, were being particularly neglected.

The Apostles decided that the thing to do was to have the Christians choose seven good men, whom everybody liked, and put them in charge of this work. "We have more than enough work to do preaching and

The First Persecution

praying," they said, "without having to give up time to distribute food."

Everybody thought this was an excellent idea and the seven men were chosen, and, to make quite sure there were no more complaints of that sort, they were all men whose language was Greek.

These seven were to help the Apostles in everything, but particularly in seeing to the distribution of goods. Luke calls them deacons. They were ordained for their work by the Apostles, not as priests — they didn't say Mass — but they were to baptize and preach as well as seeing to their own special work.

Everything went well after this, and the Church went on growing fast — even the Jewish priests of the Temple began to be converted and to come into the Church in crowds.

I wonder whether our Lady's prayers brought that about? We know she had always loved the Temple, no doubt she still went to pray there and she may very well have said some special prayers for the Temple priests.

But there were still plenty of Greek-speaking Jews in Jerusalem who had not been converted and who didn't at all like the turn things were taking.

They particularly disliked one of the deacons whose name was Stephen. He was a young man, and a very holy one, and even in those days of many miracles, his were known to be especially wonderful, and his preaching particularly successful.

They tried arguing with Stephen, but always had the worst of it, and, as I expect you have noticed, nothing is so apt to make people bad-tempered as losing an argument. So, being spiteful people, they thought of a spiteful idea, which was to pay people to spread the rumor that Stephen was speaking blasphemously of God and of Moses.

This rumor reached the ears of those Important People who had already imprisoned the Apostles and then had let them go, and who no doubt had been wondering what to do next. This, they thought, was the very thing they had been waiting for! So Stephen was pounced on and brought to the Council, and accused of blasphemy by people who knew perfectly well it wasn't true.

"Why we have heard him say," they said, "that Jesus of Nazareth will destroy this place" — they meant the Temple — "and will change the traditions Moses gave us." Just the same charge that was brought against our Lord. It's extraordinary how His followers are always finding themselves accused of just the things He was accused of. Everyone in the Council looked at Stephen, hoping to see him looking confused and guilty, but not at all — "his face was like the face of an angel."

"Are these things true?" said the High Priest.

Stephen's answer was a long speech in which he reminded them of how much God had done for His people ever since the days of Abraham. He spoke of Moses who led them out of Egypt and of how rebellion against him had broken out, of Solomon who built the Temple and of all the prophets who had foretold our Lord's coming, and he ended up like this, "Obstinate people, you are forever resisting the Holy Spirit, just as your fathers did. There was not one of the prophets they did not persecute; it was death to foretell the coming of that Just Man whom you have betrayed and murdered

The First Persecution

— *you* — who received the Law of God dictated by angels — and have not kept it!"

By "that Just Man," Stephen meant our Lord, of course, whose coming so many prophets had foretold.

The Holy Spirit can certainly make people brave, can't He? I think we ought to keep asking Him always to make us as brave as we need to be, then if we ever need to be so very brave as Stephen, we shall be all right. It is no wonder the Council and everyone who heard that speech were furious and gnashed their teeth at him.

Would you mind gnashing your teeth at me? Thank you. Mustn't a whole lot of furious old gentlemen have looked extraordinary doing that? Once again, that is just what they did at the trial of our Lord — "gnashed their teeth at Him." But Stephen looked up over their heads and said, "I see Heaven opening and the Son of Man standing at the right hand of God."

At this the whole place broke into a turmoil. Some shouted and some put their fingers in their ears so as not to hear any more, and all of them rushed at Stephen and ran him out of the town into the open ground above the city and there they stoned him.

"Stoning" was throwing large stones as hard as they could until the man they were thrown at was so hurt and broken that he died.

Stephen was praying all the time and when the great stones began to strike him he went on his knees and cried aloud, "Lord, do not count this sin against them!"

You remember that our Lord also had said, "Father forgive them, they know not what they do." We can say

The First Christians

either when anyone hurts us, then when we hurt somebody perhaps they will do the same for us.

That was how the first martyr died.

The men who stoned Stephen had taken off their coats so as to throw better and left them in charge of a young man called Saul, who thoroughly approved of what was being done. That was the very same Saul of Tarsus who was presently going to be St. Paul.

This was the beginning of the first persecution of the Church. It was so fierce that as many Christians as possible left Jerusalem and went to live in the country and in the towns round about, but the Apostles themselves stayed in Jerusalem.

And so, for the first time, the thing happened which was to happen many, many more times: the Christians who had fled from Jerusalem told their new neighbors about our Lord and His Church, so more and more people in more and more places heard about the kingdom of God on earth, and great numbers of them believed what they heard and joined the Church.

Another of the seven deacons, of whom Stephen was one, was called Philip. God had given him power to work miracles, too, to show he was telling the truth.

Philip went to Samaria and preached in one of the towns there; he healed a great many sick people, and drove devils out of many who were possessed, and made a great number of converts.

There was rejoicing all over the town because such a lot of people who had been ill and miserable were well and happy again.

Now in this same town there lived a man called Simon Magus who had been there before Philip came,

The First Persecution

and who pretended to be able to do "miracles" by magic. He had found plenty of people ready to believe him — they even called him "the great angel of God"!

Simon, of course, knew better; he knew his miracles were just tricks. But because he knew all about faked miracles, he could see at once that Philip's miracles were real. No wonder he believed all Philip told him about our Lord, and was baptized.

Meantime, Peter and John heard of what was happening in Samaria and they came down from Jerusalem to visit Philip there, just as bishops now visit the different places in their dioceses; and just as bishops do now, they confirmed Philip's converts, who were so far only baptized.

In those days the Church was so new and in so much danger that the first Christians needed every bit of special encouragement they could have, which is why there were so many more miracles then than there are now. At Confirmation the Holy Spirit used to show that He had come by giving the people being confirmed visible gifts besides the invisible ones of grace that He always brings to all of us. One of them might be given the power to work miracles of healing and another might begin to speak in a language he had not learned, and another might begin to prophesy.

Prophesying was saying something the Holy Spirit put into your mind which you wouldn't have known about otherwise — either something about what was going to happen in the future, or a new understanding of something you had been taught.

The gift of speaking a language you hadn't learned must have been quite exciting, but there was a catch about it! Unless you had another gift as well, the gift of interpretation, you didn't understand what you were saying. You knew you were praising God, but the words didn't mean anything to you. Isn't that odd?

You see, this gift wasn't given to make it easy for the first Christians to teach foreigners wherever they went in the world, as we often think. They didn't really need it for that, because nearly anywhere they went people spoke some kind of Greek.

Perhaps when Thomas got to India he spoke the language of the people there, but in the ordinary way the purpose of this gift was just to surprise unbelievers into stopping and listening.

We know all this about the gift of tongues, as it is called, from Paul. He wrote a letter to some of his converts, long after this, of course, which we call the Epistle to the Corinthians, in which he tells them that though this gift from the Holy Spirit is good, they ought not to use it in Church too much, and not at all unless there is someone there who can interpret what is being said. And he tells them that the gift of prophecy is a much better one because that is useful to people who have the Faith, not just to heathens.

Well, to get back to Peter and John who had come to confirm Philip's converts. The Holy Spirit came to them and gave them these wonderful gifts, and when Simon Magus saw it, he was very much impressed, but not at all in the right way. He said to Peter, "Make me able to give the Holy Spirit, too, and I will pay you well."

Peter was very indignant at this, as well he might be. "Keep your money to perish with you," he said.

The First Persecution

"You, who have thought that the free gift of God can be bought. You have a bad conscience: repent and pray for forgiveness, you are a slave of sin."

Simon said, "Pray for me to the Lord that no harm may come to me." And, do you know, we never hear another word in the Acts of the Apostles about Simon.

The sin of simony, which is selling holy things, is called after him, but I always hope he was really sorry and that he got safely to Heaven in the end.

After the Apostles had finished their visit and gone back to Jerusalem, an angel appeared to Philip and told him to go out on the road that went through the desert to Gaza.

Away went Philip, and on the road he saw a grand open carriage of the sort called a chariot with a man sitting in it reading. He was an Ethiopian and treasurer to the queen of that country. He believed in God, though he was not a Jew, and he had been up to the Temple to worship and now was on his way home again. What he was reading was the book of the prophet Isaiah, which is full of prophecies of our Lord, and especially of the Passion.

The Holy Spirit told Philip to go up to the chariot and keep beside it. So Philip ran up and as he came near heard the man in it reading aloud to himself. "Can you understand what you are reading?" asked Philip. "How can I," said the treasurer, "without someone to show me what it means?" And he asked Philip please to come up into the chariot and sit by him and explain who it was that Isaiah was talking about.

So Philip and the treasurer rode along together, and Philip taught so well and the treasurer was so eager to

The First Christians

learn that presently when they came to a pool of water, he pointed it out to Philip and said, "Could I be baptized now?"

"Yes," said Philip, "if you really believe with all your heart, you may."

The treasurer answered, "I believe that Jesus Christ is the Son of God." He had the chariot stopped and he and Philip went down to the pool and Philip baptized him.

Wouldn't you love to know what happened when he got home? But Luke doesn't say a word about it — perhaps he didn't know either. So there is no way of finding out until we get to Heaven and can ask Philip or the treasurer.

As for Philip, Luke says he turned up next in Azotus near the Mediterranean and

The First Persecution

went through all the villages about there until he came to Caesarea. There he seems to have settled down with his family.

Chapter Four

Saul

(Acts 9)

Do you remember the young man called Saul who looked after the coats for the people who stoned Stephen? He was a learned young Pharisee from Tarsus, a city in what was called Cilicia then, but which we would now call part of Turkey.

Saul had come to Jerusalem to study under the rabbis there, and one thing he had learned was a bitter hatred for our Lord and all His followers. Seeing Stephen stoned to death had not made him feel any differently about it; he was determined to go on persecuting the first Christians until there were none left anywhere.

Saul heard that there were a lot of Christians in Damascus, a city about 150 miles from Jerusalem. First of all he went to the High Priest to get letters to the chief Jews in Damascus saying that it was all right for him to arrest Christians and bring them back to Jerusalem.

Then he found a party of people bound for Damascus and set out on his journey with them. Going on a journey by yourself was very dangerous in those

The First Christians

days — the more people you had with you the better, because there were robbers who watched lonely parts of the road and attacked any travelers they could find going along the road by themselves or in very small groups.

It took four or five days to go to Damascus from Jerusalem — I daresay if everyone had had a fast horse to ride it would have been less, but as some would be riding and some walking, the party had to go as slowly as if they had all been on foot.

No one attacked Saul's party as far as we know, and they came at last quite close to Damascus, Saul still full of plans for catching Christians. Suddenly, without any warning, a great light shone around them, far brighter than the sun. Saul fell down on the ground and heard a voice say, "Saul, Saul, why do you persecute me?" This was our Lord's voice speaking to Saul and telling him that persecuting His Church was just the same as persecuting Him.

Luke doesn't say here that Saul saw our Lord as well as hearing His voice, but when Saul tells the story himself, later on, he makes it clear that he did see Him.

So there was Saul, still lying on the ground, with all his ideas turning upside down in his head. "Who are you, Lord?" he said.

"I am Jesus, whom you are persecuting," our Lord answered. "It is hard for you to kick against the goad."

A goad is a stick with a very sharp point, used for prodding donkeys to make them go faster of course, if they kick back at it, it just pricks all the harder. Our Lord meant that He had been pricking Saul's conscience with His grace, making him wonder whether it

Saul

was really right to persecute His followers, but Saul had refused to attend.

Saul, all dazed and shaking, said, "Lord, what do you want me to do?"

Our Lord said, "Get up and go, Saul, into the city, and there you will be told what you are to do."

The people with Saul were very astonished and very puzzled: they had seen the bright light and heard a voice speaking, but had not seen anyone and could not understand what was said. When Saul struggled up from the ground they found he was quite blind, which made everything seem more extraordinary still.

They led him into the city of Damascus, and he went to the house belonging to a man called Judas in Strait Street and lodged there. He was still blind and so he stayed for three days, and he didn't eat or drink anything all that time.

In the meantime, our Lord appeared in a vision to one of the Christians in Damascus. His name was Ananias but he has nothing to do with the wicked Ananias who lied about the estate he had sold, any more than the Judas in Damascus had anything to do with Judas who betrayed our Lord. Ananias and Judas were just ordinary names then, as John and James are now.

"Ananias," said our Lord in the vision.

"Here I am, Lord!" said Ananias.

Our Lord told him to go to Judas's house in Strait Street, and ask for a man lodging there called Saul.

"He is praying," our Lord went on, "and he has had a vision of you coming in to lay your hands on him and cure him of blindness."

The First Christians

This puzzled Ananias very much and he seems to have wondered if our Lord really knew what He was doing. "Lord," he said, "a lot of people have told me about this man and the way he has persecuted your Church in Jerusalem, and now he has come here with authority to carry us away to Jerusalem to be put in prison."

Our Lord didn't argue about it. He just said, "Go on your errand. This is a man I have chosen to bring My Name before the heathen and their rulers and before the Jews, too. I have not told him yet what great things he will have to suffer for my Name's sake."

So away went Ananias in search of Saul, and as soon as he came into the room where Saul was, Ananias went up to Saul and laid his hands on him. "Brother Saul," he said, "I have been sent by the Lord Jesus who appeared to you on your journey to this city. You are to receive your sight and be filled with the Holy Spirit."

Immediately, Saul could see perfectly well, and he was baptized by Ananias, and had something to eat and then felt quite all right again.

For some days after this he stayed with the Christians in Damascus. He went about preaching, as they did, and told everyone that Jesus is the Son of God. Naturally, this puzzled people a good deal. "Surely," they said, "this is the same man who was so furious with the Christians in Jerusalem? Didn't he come here especially to arrest any he could find? What can this mean?"

But Saul was inspired, and only preached more strongly than ever, showing the Jews that our Lord was really the Christ.

Saul

After this, as we know, not from Luke, but from Saul's own writings, he went and made a very long retreat indeed — about three years long — in Arabia.

This was the time when our Lord prepared him for the great mission He had given him: Saul was to be an Apostle, as important as the first Twelve. Our Lord spent three years training them, too, so it looks as if that is the time needed to make an Apostle, doesn't it?

After this he came back to Damascus. The Jews there found him worse than ever: he wouldn't stop preaching; he always won arguments, and everyone was listening to him. At last they could bear it no longer, so they made a plot to kill him.

Saul and the other Christians heard about it and wondered what on earth to do. Damascus was a city enclosed by very high walls, and the only ways of getting out of it were by the gates cut in these walls.

Each gate, they knew, was being watched day and night. The plotters thought they were bound to catch Saul either in the city, or trying to leave it.

It was a very awkward situation indeed. But somebody had a good idea — I wish we knew who it was — and this idea worked splendidly. Saul was put into a hamper, one of those big baskets with a lid that fastens. They are used for vegetables and carrier pigeons and laundry and all sorts of things still; I am sure you have seen one.

When he was nicely packed in, they put a rope around the hamper and let it down from the top of the wall to the ground outside.

It was really very clever, because it wasn't likely anyone would see the hamper being let down (I am sure

The First Christians

they did it at night) and if anyone did see it, he wasn't likely to guess Saul was inside.

So that was how Saul got safely away from the city. Once outside he made his way back to Jerusalem and went to look for his fellow Christians there.

News of Saul's conversion must have come to Jerusalem long before, but perhaps it had seemed too good to be true, or they had forgotten. Anyway, no Christians would have anything to do with him, until he found Barnabas, who knew all about him, and took him and introduced him to Peter and to James, the bishop of Jerusalem.

Barnabas told them all about how our Lord had spoken to Saul on his way to Damascus and how boldly he had preached there. After that it was all right, and Saul stayed a fortnight with Peter and joined in preaching about our Lord in Jerusalem.

But there must have been something about Saul, because presently another plot was started against him.

When this was discovered it was decided that it would be a good idea if he went home to his own city of Tarsus for a while. Some of the Christians went with him as far as Caesarea where he could get a ship to take him the rest of the way.

If you want to know how he went, you will find Caesarea on the map printed at each end of this book. He sailed north from there to his city, Tarsus, which was the capital of Cilicia.

Chapter Five

Peter's Vision
(Acts 9 cont., 10, 11, 12)

In the meantime, apart from the plot against Saul, the first Christians in Palestine were having a much more peaceful time than they were used to.

This was because the Roman Emperor was being so difficult that everyone was worrying so much about what he would do next and had no time to bother with the Christians. So the Church grew and increased quickly.

Peter, like any other bishop, used to travel about, seeing how the Church was getting on in all the different places round about Jerusalem, and confirming people who so far had only been baptized.

On one of his journeys he came to Lydda, a town near the coast. There he heard of a man called Aeneas who was paralyzed and who had not been able to leave his bed for eight whole years.

Peter went to see him. "Aeneas," he said, "the Lord Jesus Christ is going to make you well again now — get up and make your bed!"

Aeneas popped up out of bed at once, perfectly cured, and of course everyone who heard of it came to see him and to hear all about it. Then they wanted to know about our Lord and when Peter had told them, they joined the Church too.

While Peter was still in Lydda, messengers came to him from Joppe (which we call Jaffa nowadays), a port on the seacoast a few miles away. These messengers said that a woman called Tabitha, who lived in Joppe, had just died. Would Peter please come at once? Off went Peter straightaway and they took him up to Tabitha's room where her body was lying on the bed.

In the room there were a lot of poor widows, all crying like anything and saying they did not know what they were going to do without Tabitha — she had always been so good to them and had made them coats and dresses — they kept showing these to Peter who I daresay felt rather bothered by all this fuss. He told them please to leave him alone with Tabitha, and when they were gone he knelt down by the bed and prayed. Then turning toward the body, Peter said, "Get up, Tabitha!"

Tabitha opened her eyes, saw Peter, and sat up. He gave her his hand and helped her up and then called for everybody to come back into the room. You can imagine the excitement there was then.

Tabitha is a rather nice name; I don't know why we so often give it to cats and so seldom to people. It means "gazelle."

This miracle led to still more conversions and the Church grew and grew. To help with it all Peter stayed on in Joppe for some time after this, lodging with a tanner whose name was Simon.

A tanner is a man whose trade is turning raw hides into dressed leather fit for shoes and saddles and all the

Peter's Vision

other things leather is used for. If you have ever been over a tannery, or even near one, you will know that it is rather a smelly business, but then Peter was a fisherman, and fish don't always smell too good, so perhaps he didn't mind.

In these very early days of our Lord's Church there had been very few converts who were not Jews, and even the Apostles didn't realize yet that it no longer mattered in the least whether you were a Jew or not, and that the Jewish laws about what sort of animals were to be eaten, and all those kinds of rules, were no longer binding.

It was difficult for them to realize this because they were so used to thinking of themselves as the Chosen People of God. But God wanted to make it quite plain that anyone at all could come into His Church, and the tenth chapter of Acts, which is where we have got to now, is all about how He did it.

Peter was still at Joppe and Saul was on his way home to Tarsus, but the story doesn't start with either of them; it starts with a Roman officer called Cornelius who was stationed at Caesarea, the port from which Saul sailed.

Cornelius was a centurion, which means that he was a solider in command of a hundred men, and he belonged to what was called the Italian Cohort. A cohort was about six hundred men.

The Romans got their soldiers from any place that was handy — most of those in Palestine were probably from the countries round about there. But the Roman governor lived in Caesarea and he liked to have a regiment with him made up of Italians, and under Roman

The First Christians

officers. This centurion called Cornelius belonged to one of the great families of Rome. He had been brought up a pagan, of course, but in Palestine he had learned about the one God of the Jews, and that was the God Cornelius worshipped, and so did all his household. Altogether Cornelius was a very good sort of man: he said his prayers and gave as much money as he could to the poor.

At three o'clock one afternoon, Cornelius had a vision: He saw an angel come into his room.

"Cornelius," said the angel.

Cornelius was badly frightened. Wars and wounds he could take in his stride, no doubt, but seeing an angel was quite another matter.

"What is it, lord?" he said, looking at the angel in terror.

"Your prayers and alms-deeds are recorded in God's sight," said the angel reassuringly, "and now you are to send men to Joppe to bring you Simon who is called Peter. He is lodging with a tanner who is also called Simon, and the house is by the sea. Peter will tell you what God wants you to do."

Then the angel left him. Cornelius called a trustworthy soldier and two of his household servants and told them what had happened and sent them off to Joppe to find Peter.

They didn't reach Joppe until the afternoon of the next day. While they were on their way, Peter went up onto the flat roof of Simon's house to pray.

In Palestine people use the roofs of their houses as an extra room — a good place to go to if you want to be by yourself.

Peter's Vision

It was about noon and as Peter said his prayers he kept hoping dinner would soon be ready, because he was so hungry. All at once he forgot both his prayers and his dinner: like Cornelius, he was seeing a vision.

What he saw was an enormous sheet being let down from the sky to the earth. It seemed as if hands in Heaven were holding it by its four corners and the middle of the sheet was full of something — as it came lower and at last touched the earth, he could see what was in it. Animals! Wild beasts and birds and lizards and snakes, a whole zoo all mixed up together in this one great sheet.

The First Christians

As Peter looked at them in astonishment he heard a voice say, "Get up, Peter, kill some of those and eat!"

Peter was horrified. He could see that many of the beasts in the sheet were forbidden to the Jews as not clean food for them. "It cannot be, Lord," he said, "never in my life have I eaten unclean animals."

The great voice spoke again, "It is not for you to call anything unclean when God has made it clean." This happened three times and then the sheet was drawn up to Heaven again.

Peter sat on the roof, wondering what on earth it meant, but God said to him, "There are three men at the gate asking for you. Go down to them and do what they want you to. It is quite all right: I have sent them."

Peter went down from the roof and sure enough, there were the three messengers from Cornelius asking for him. "Here I am," said Peter. "What do you want with me?"

They told him about Cornelius and how an angel had come to tell him what God wanted him to do.

So Peter asked them to come into the house (I do hope there was enough dinner for everybody!) and they stayed there overnight. The next day they set off with Peter for Caesarea and some of the Jewish Christians from Joppe went with them.

Peter understood now what his vision had meant — that the old rules about what was clean and unclean didn't count any more and that God wanted him to go with people who were not Jews and to preach in a Gentile's house.

On the following day, when they all arrived in Caesarea, Cornelius met them at the door of his house

Peter's Vision

and bowed down to the ground before Peter, to show his reverence for him.

"Stand up," said Peter hastily, "I am only a man like you."

Cornelius had collected all the friends and relations he could to welcome Peter. When they went into the house and Peter saw this crowd, he knew the Jewish Christians he had brought with him would be wondering if it could possibly be all right for them to go in and sit and talk with all these Gentiles, so he said, "You know that we Jews do not visit people who are not Jews, and if we do, we are thought to be unclean. But God has been showing me that this is no longer right, and that we ought not to speak of any man as unclean. So when I was sent for, I came at once. Tell me what you require of me."

Cornelius told them about his vision and how an angel had told him to send for Peter. He thanked Peter for coming and then asked him to please tell them whatever God wanted them to hear.

"I see clearly," said Peter, "that God welcomes men of every race so long as they are trying to please Him." Then he told them about our Lord: how He had gone about curing sick people and driving devils away, and how Peter himself and the other Apostles were witnesses of what He had done, and how He had been crucified at last but had risen again and had sent the Apostles to preach about Him. Peter also told them how the prophets had spoken of our Lord and that everyone who had faith in Him was to find forgiveness for his sins.

Before he had finished speaking the Holy Spirit came down on them all and as a sign of it they began to

The First Christians

speak in foreign languages, just as the Apostles had at Pentecost.

The Jewish Christians who had come with Peter from Joppe were astonished, almost shocked, to see that this could happen to people who were not Jews. But Peter understood very well what God wanted. He said, "Who will grudge us water to baptize these people who have received the Holy Spirit, just as we did?"

So Cornelius and his friends and relations were all baptized and Peter stayed on with them for some days to tell them more about our Lord and His Church.

When Peter ended his visit to Cornelius's house at Caesarea, he came back to Jerusalem.

News of what had been happening had arrived ahead of him and the Jewish Christians were very upset about it. As soon as they saw Peter they asked, "Why did you go and visit men who are not Jews and even sit and eat with them?"

So Peter patiently told them the whole story all over again: how he had had the vision of a great sheet full of all kinds of animals let down from Heaven and about Cornelius's vision and how he, Peter, had gone with Cornelius's messengers because God had told him to and how the Holy Spirit had come down on Cornelius and his friends and relations just as it had happened to the Apostles on the day of Pentecost.

"And now," he ended, "if God chose to give them His gifts just as He did to us, who was I to try to prevent Him?"

"Why, then," said the Jewish Christians, in great surprise, "God must have given life giving repentance to these people who are not Jews, too!"

Peter's Vision

For the time being that settled it, but, as you will see, only for the time being.

In the meantime, some of the first Christians who had left Jerusalem during the first persecutions had gone a long way. Some had settled in Phoenicia on the northwest of Palestine, some were on the island of Cyprus and still others in Antioch, the capital of Syria.

In all these places they found Jewish neighbors and these they told about our Lord, but none of them thought of inviting the pagan Greeks to join the Church except some Christians from Cyprus and the town of Cyrene. These men went to Antioch and there preached to the pagans. I don't know how they guessed that it was all right to do so, whether God told them specially, or what, but anyhow they did, and a great many of the pagans were converted.

When the Apostles heard of this they sent Barnabas to Antioch to help. Barnabas was delighted to find so many and such good converts, but he could see that still more help was needed. So off he went to Tarsus to find Saul. He found him and brought him back to Antioch and both of them stayed there a whole year, there was so much to do.

There is one particularly interesting thing that Luke tells us about Antioch — it was the very first place where we were called Christians. I think this was because it was the first place where most of the converts had been pagans. In other places followers of our Lord were thought of as some special kind of Jews, but in Antioch they could see that that wasn't true.

In those days, of course, there was just one kind of Christian, and every Christian was a member of the

The First Christians

Catholic Church, the exact same Church to which we belong. So wherever you see *Christian*, whether in this book or in the Acts of the Apostles, just remember it means the same as *Catholic*.

While Saul and Barnabas were still at Antioch a visitor arrived. His name was Agabus and he had the gift of prophecy. He had come to tell them that he knew by this gift that there was going to be a great famine which would affect the whole world.

Luke doesn't say that Agabus said the famine would come first to the country round about Jerusalem and only later to Antioch, but he must have said something like that, because it was decided that the Christians in Antioch would take up a collection and send it to the Christians in Jerusalem. And so they did, each giving whatever he could afford, and the collection was given to Saul and Barnabas to take to Jerusalem.

Now there was trouble starting in Jerusalem again.

Herod, the same Herod who had mocked our Lord and sent Him to Pilate in a white garment, was very anxious to please the Jews, who were none too fond of him. He heard how bitter many of them were about the Christians, so he arrested James the Apostle, John's brother, and cut his head off. This was a great success from his point of view since the Jewish rulers were delighted. So he took Peter, too, and put him in prison.

So James (the brother of John) who had been beheaded by Herod, was the first of the Apostles to die as a martyr.

He was the first to go to Heaven to join our Lord; and his brother John, who wrote the fourth Gospel, was the last of all the Twelve to get there.

Peter's Vision

Meanwhile, Peter was in prison. Why didn't Herod kill him straight away, too? Because it was the time of the Paschal feast, one of the great feasts of the Jews, and he wanted to wait until it was over before dealing with Peter.

Herod didn't mean there to be any nonsense about Peter escaping again, as he and John had before, so he ordered twelve soldiers to guard him. These worked in sets of four, and each four were on duty for three hours. Two of them stood in front of the door of Peter's cell and two more were chained to him, one on each side. You wouldn't think anything could be safer than that, would you? But the whole Church was praying as hard as ever they could for Peter, and this is how God answered their prayers.

In the middle of the night, when Peter and the two soldiers chained to him were asleep, and the other two soldiers were standing on guard outside the door, an angel appeared in the cell. He struck Peter on the side to wake him up. Peter opened his eyes to find a bright light shining about him and the angel bending over him.

"Quick," said the angel. "Get up!"

Peter stumbled up, still half asleep, and the chains that bound him to the two soldiers fell off.

"Get ready," said the angel. "Put your shoes on." And when Peter had done that, the angel continued, "Now, put your cloak around you and follow me."

The door of the cell opened by itself and Peter followed the angel through it and out of the prison, past two lots of guards, who never saw them at all. Lastly, the iron gate in front of the prison opened for them and they walked out and along the street. All this time sleepy Peter thought he was seeing a vision, but when the angel left him, he woke up completely to find he really was out in the streets of Jerusalem.

"Now I know for certain," he said to himself, "that God has sent His angel to set me free."

He stood for a moment wondering where to go, and then set off for a house belonging to the mother of a young man called Mark — the same Mark who wrote one of the Gospels.

Inside the house there were a great many people, all praying as hard as they could for Peter. When he knocked on the door a girl called Rhoda went to see who was there, but when she heard Peter's voice through the door, she was so excited she didn't open it! Instead she ran back to the room where everyone was praying and told them that Peter was at the gate.

"Nonsense!" they said.

"It is Peter!" said Rhoda.

"Perhaps," someone suggested, "it is his guardian angel." And they finally went to the door, where Peter was still knocking, and opened it.

When they saw who was there, they stood back in astonishment and Peter came in, holding up his hand to tell them not to make a noise. He told them all that had happened and asked them to let James know about it. This was the other Apostle James, the one who was bishop of Jerusalem, and our Lord's cousin, of course, not the one who had just had his head cut off.

Then, as it seemed better for Peter to be as far away as possible before he was missed from the prison, he left Jerusalem at once.

Peter's Vision

Luke doesn't tell us where he went, but most people think he went to Antioch and was bishop there for some time before he went to Rome.

When it was time to change Peter's guards, very early in the morning, there was a terrible fuss in the prison. Where in the world was Peter? Herod was furious, of course, and had a terrific search made for him. But it was no use. So he had Peter's guards put to death. I hope they were allowed, somehow or other, to go to Heaven, because it was really rather hard on them!

After this, Herod, still in a very bad temper, left Jerusalem and went to Caesarea, where he was going to hold great festivities in honor of the Roman Emperor.

Besides feeling thoroughly silly over Peter's escape, he was angry for some reason with the people of Tyre and Sidon, the two main cities of Phoenicia. The people of these cities wanted very badly to make friends with him again, because a famine was starting in their country, and they depended for much of their food on Palestine. This was part of the famine foretold by the prophet Agabus, and it was being felt in Palestine, too, but no doubt not so badly.

Well, the people from Tyre and Sidon came to Caesarea to see Herod. They made friends (by bribes, I expect) with Herod's chamberlain, Blastus, and he arranged for them to see Herod during the festivities. Herod had dressed up in his very best and most royal robes for the occasion and he sat on a raised platform to speak to them, looking as grand as he possibly could.

The people from Tyre and Sidon thought a little flattery would do no harm. They shouted, "It is not a man but a god who speaks to us!"

The First Christians

Herod thought that was fine. He was all for being considered a god, but the real God had suddenly had enough of Herod. He sent an angel to strike him there and then with a horrible disease. No one saw the angel, but they saw Herod suddenly crumple up in his grand clothes and saw him carried away, not looking in the least like a god. He died a few days later, and that was the end of him.

Chapter Six

Saul's First Great Journey
(Acts 12 cont., 13, 14)

Meanwhile, Saul and Barnabas had brought the money that they had collected in Antioch to Jerusalem, and having handed it over and heard all the news about Peter, they started back to Antioch again, taking Mark with them.

In charge of the church at Antioch were Simon Niger, Lucius of Cyrene, and Manahen. Manahen had been brought up with Herod's son, and you would have thought he would have learned all kinds of wickedness in Herod's palace, but he had become a Christian and now he and the other two were bishops or priests — we don't know which — at Antioch.

Last time we heard of Peter he was probably on his way to Antioch, but if so, at the time we have come to now, he must have been on a journey to some other place, for Luke says nothing about him being there when Saul and Barnabas arrived from Jerusalem.

What he does tell us is that Simon Niger, Lucius of Cyrene, and Manahen were fasting and offering Mass when the Holy Spirit said to them, "I must have Saul and Barnabas consecrated for the special work I want

The First Christians

them to do." So Saul and Barnabas were consecrated bishops and set out to convert the non-Jewish world, for this was what the Holy Spirit wanted of them.

That doesn't mean that they were not to say anything about our Lord to the Jews; not at all — the Jews were still to have first chance wherever they went, but as soon as they had been given this first chance, Saul and Barnabas were to begin preaching to everybody else.

On this their first missionary journey, they went to Seleucia, the port for Antioch, and there boarded a ship which was sailing for Cyprus, and Mark (who wrote the Gospel) went with them.

In the Acts, Mark is sometimes called John Mark or just John, but I am calling him Mark all the time, because it is less confusing. At that time it was quite ordinary for a Jew to have one name for his Jewish friends and another for people who did not speak Aramaic, and that's why so many people in the New Testament have more than one name.

I expect one reason they went to Cyprus was that Barnabas had been born there and wanted to see that all his friends and relations had a chance to hear about our Lord.

There were quite a lot of Christians on Cyprus already; some of those who had fled from the first persecutions in Jerusalem had gone there, and they had made new converts after they arrived. Still, there were plenty more people who were Jewish or pagan.

The Apostles landed at Salamis, at the eastern end of the island, and set out to walk the one hundred and forty miles to the western end, stopping, of course, to

Saul's First Great Journey

preach and instruct people wherever they saw a good chance to do so.

I have been on Cyprus, too, and found it a pleasant sort of island with very few trees and lots and lots of goats. In the Apostles' time there were plenty of trees, and, I expect, fewer goats — anyone will tell you that goats and trees don't go together, because the goats will eat the trees and then the trees die and the goats don't mind a bit — they just go ahead and eat the grass they were supposed to eat in the first place.

I like goats all the same, and I daresay Saul did too, because his trade was making tents out of goats' hair. He went on doing this even when he was being a missionary bishop, because then he could pay his own way and no one could say he was making money out of converting people.

And I suspect he had another reason: while he was sitting working away on a tent must have been a good time to talk to people and tell them about our Lord. It must have been a good time, for dictating letters, too.

The First Christians

The Epistles of St. Paul, you know, are all letters he wrote to be read in the churches he had started in different places. He wrote to remind them of what he had taught them, to explain something else they wanted to know about, or to warn them of special dangers. We know he usually dictated them because he often says at the end of the letter that now he is going to finish it off and sign it in his own handwriting, so that they can be sure it is from him.

Luke tells us nothing about Saul and Barnabas's journey across Cyprus, he only tells us what happened in the last city they came to, right at the west of the island. This was a city called Paphos, and it was where the Roman governor of the island lived. He was called Sergius Paulus and was a good, sensible sort of man. But he had made friends with a man who was neither good nor sensible. This was a Jew whose Jewish name was Bar Josue and whose Greek name was Elymas, which means "magician."

When Sergius Paulus heard that Saul and Barnabas were coming, he sent a message to them saying that he would like to hear what they had to say. This didn't suit Elymas at all. When the Apostles came he argued with them and did his very best to turn the governor against them. But the Holy Spirit had told Saul what to do.

He looked hard at Elymas and said, "Child of the devil, full of tricks and slyness, enemy of honesty, will you never stop trying to twist the straight path to God? See if you do not feel the hand of God now: you are going to be blind for a time."

No sooner had Saul said this than Elymas did go quite blind and he groped about looking for someone to

Saul's First Great Journey

lead him by the hand. So all his trying to turn Sergius Paulus away from the Apostles' teaching had just the opposite effect. After seeing such a wonderful thing as this, the governor listened to Saul and Barnabas all the more eagerly, and he believed what they told him and came into the Church.

We can imagine the excitement in Cyprus over no less a person than the Roman governor being converted, but Luke doesn't say a word about it. He does tell us in this chapter that Saul's Roman name was Paul, and he calls him Paul from now on. And I am very glad of it; I can't tell you how often I have written Paul and then had to rub it out and write Saul instead. Some people think Saul had always had two names (like Mark), but others think he took Paul as his name because he was so pleased at having converted Sergius Paulus. That's another thing we can't know for sure until we get to Heaven and can ask him.

From Paphos, Paul and Barnabas and Mark sailed to a place called Perge in the country of Pamiphilia, about a hundred miles away. It was part of the land we call Turkey now. When they got there, Mark left them and went back to Jerusalem. We don't know why, but we do know that Paul was very much annoyed with him for going, which shows that even saints can't always manage to agree with each other.

From Perge, Paul and Barnabas set out for a place called Antioch-in-Pisidia. This sounds like a strange name, but there were several Antiochs, so it had to be called that to distinguish it from the other ones, just as if you say you come from Springfield, someone is sure to ask you which Springfield — the one in Massachusetts,

The First Christians

the one in Illinois, or the one in Ohio? Luke just says they went there, as if it was as simple as taking a cab, but it was really a terrific journey. They had to travel on foot for a whole week, and the first part of the journey was through mountains — up, over passes where there were still snowdrifts and down through wild rocky canyons with torrents running through them.

There were bandits living in the mountains, too, looking out for travelers to rob. The Apostles must have been quite a tough pair, mustn't they?

After they had passed the mountains they came out onto barren upland country with very few people about except shepherds. These, Paul will have been glad to see, lived in just the same kind of black goats' hair tents as he made. They passed great lakes, too, with crowds of storks standing beside them.

The first Saturday after they finished this journey and arrived in Antioch-in-Pisidia, they went, as they usually did, to the synagogue for the weekly service.

The Jews in charge of the synagogue saw that there were two strangers among them and, as the custom was, sent them a polite message saying they would be glad to listen to anything they had to say after the regular service.

"If you have anything encouraging to tell us," said the message, "let us hear it."

Paul didn't have to be asked twice. Up he stood and began to speak. Scholars (who can discover the most astonishing things) say that Paul was a small, insignificant looking little man, and ugly, too, so most likely the congregation didn't expect much from him.

However, he started off just as they liked a sermon to begin, by reminding them of their own beginnings

Saul's First Great Journey

and history — how God had chosen them, and what wonderful things He had done for them since. You can imagine them all settling back and hoping it wouldn't go on too long. And then Paul came to King David and he said, "It is of this man's descendants, as it was promised by God, that He has given us a Savior, Jesus."

Now they sat up! Paul went on to tell them of John the Baptist who had prepared the way for our Lord and of how His own people had had Jesus put to death by Pilate, not realizing who He was, and of how He had been buried and had risen again and of all the people who had seen Him alive after his death.

"Here is news for you," Paul ended. "Forgiveness of sins is offered to you through Him; the things you could never be forgiven under the Old Law, you now can be forgiven through Him."

Everybody was very much impressed, and Paul and Barnabas were asked to come back and tell them more next Saturday.

But many of the congregation were too interested to wait a whole week; they followed Paul and Barnabas out of the synagogue and walked home with them, asking questions all the way. And when next Saturday came there was an enormous crowd waiting for them at the synagogue. "Almost the whole city," says Luke, "had come to hear them."

The Jewish leaders, when they saw this, were furious. Two wandering preachers had collected all these people when they, who had worked here for years, had made only a few converts! So they began to argue against Paul and Barnabas and to try to turn the people against them.

The First Christians

"Very well," said the Apostles when they saw this, "we were bound to preach to you first, but now as you show you are not fit for eternal life, we will go and preach to the people of the city who are not Jews."

The pagan people were very glad to hear it was their turn now and great numbers of them were converted, so that the Church spread far and wide through all that country.

But the Jewish leaders, determined to get rid of the Apostles, thought of various grand ladies, pagan born, who had learned from them to worship the true God. They persuaded these ladies to tell their important pagan husbands that the Apostles were dangerous, fanatical men who were upsetting everybody in the name of religion. This was the last thing the rich men of the city wanted, so they started a persecution against the Apostles, saying they must go . . . or else.

Paul and Barnabas probably felt it was time to be on their way anyhow, the Church was well established already. But to show what they thought of such treatment they shook the dust of the city off their feet as they left — do you remember our Lord telling His disciples to do that, long before, if they preached in a city and were not listened to?

But the young church of Antioch-in-Pisidia flourished, full of the Holy Spirit and of joy. They were very sorry to see Paul and Barnabas go, but they were much too happy about belonging to the kingdom of God to be at all worried about whether they too would be persecuted, or about anything else.

After Paul and Barnabas were driven out of Antioch-in-Pisidia by the Jews who had not been converted, they

Saul's First Great Journey

went to a city called Iconium about sixty miles away. Here they preached first in the synagogue, as usual, and here also a great number of people, both Jews and heathens, believed all they said and joined the Church. But here, as kept happening everywhere, some of the Jews were very much upset when they realized that Gentiles who joined the Church were not to be taught that they must keep the Jewish Law. They simply could not get used to the idea that this didn't matter any more.

So presently there was trouble about it at Iconium as there had been in so many other places, and some of the leading Jews persuaded the Gentile rulers that the Apostles were just people out to make trouble in the name of religion, and between them they made a plot to kill Paul and Barnabas by stoning them.

The new church in Iconium was already well established and able to stand on its own feet, so when the Apostles heard what was being planned they left that city and went on to the cities of Lystra and Derbe, which were thirty miles or so to the south. There was no synagogue in either of these cities, so I expect they thought that in Lystra and Derbe and in the country around them they would have a clear field.

At Lystra something happened which will remind you of a story in an earlier chapter of the Acts, a story that everybody likes.

Among the crowd listening to Paul preaching at Lystra was a lame man who had never been able to walk in his whole life. Paul, looking at him as he preached, saw that he was believing him, and was ready to belong to our Lord, so he broke off preaching and spoke to him. "Stand up on your feet!" he said, and the lame man

The First Christians

jumped up and began to walk. That is very like the story of Peter and the crippled man who jumped, isn't it? But the rest of the story is not at all like it because the people who saw this new miracle were pagans, who worshipped the old false gods of Rome.

So what did they do but start shouting in their own language, "The gods have come down to us looking like men!"

They thought Barnabas, who was a big, handsome man, must be Jupiter, the greatest of their gods, and that Paul must be Mercury, the messenger of the gods, because he did most of the talking. I don't think the Apostles realized what was going on until the priests from the temple of Jupiter arrived with bulls covered in garlands of flowers, ready to be sacrificed to the two "gods."

As soon as they saw this, Paul and Barnabas ran out into the crowd tearing their clothes (which was a way the Jews had of showing they were very much upset) and shouting to everybody, "What are you doing? We are only men, just as you are — the whole point of what we have been telling you is that you are not to do silly things like this! We are trying to teach you to worship only the living God who made the sky and the earth and everything that is in them!"

And they went on to explain that even though in the past God had left them without special knowledge of Himself, yet He had given them the rain to make their crops grow and the four seasons, so that they could plant and gather their harvests.

Poor Paul and Barnabas! They talked and talked and, I have no doubt, got very hot and hoarse, and even

Saul's First Great Journey

so only just managed to prevent the priests of Jupiter from killing their bulls as a sacrifice to them.

Don't you think that is rather a funny story? I do, and I have an idea (which is probably nonsense) that Barnabas thought so too, and that when he and Paul and Luke met, it was Barnabas who told the story, and that he and Luke laughed and laughed about it and Paul couldn't imagine why. I wonder what you think about it?

After this very odd beginning, the Apostles made many converts at Lystra, but would you believe it, some of those tiresome Jews who had made so much trouble for them at Iconium and Antioch-in-Pisidia followed them to Lystra and started making more trouble there.

They had meant to have the Apostles stoned at Iconium; now at Lystra, they succeeded in persuading the people who were not yet converted that Paul and Barnabas were just trying to upset everything in the name of religion, their favorite charge.

They caught Paul, and they did stone him, and when they were sure the great stones had killed him, they dragged his body outside the city and left it there. Some of the new Christians stood in a ring around it, thinking, no doubt, that when everything was quiet they could take it away and have a proper funeral.

But God had far too much work for Paul to do to allow him to die yet, so to their amazement, they presently saw Paul stand up, not only not dead, but apparently quite all right — no bones broken, even.

He walked calmly back to the city with them, and he was probably the only person there who wasn't really surprised — by this time I think he must have used up every bit of surprise he had.

The First Christians

The next day Paul and Barnabas left Lystra and went on to Derbe. Here they stayed for some time and had great success and no trouble as far as we know.

I can't help wondering what happened when the Jews who thought they had killed Paul found out that they hadn't, and what they made of it.

When the Church was well established in Derbe, they came back to Lystra, and from there went to Iconium and Antioch-in-Pisidia, in each of these places ordaining priests and leaving fine churches flourishing.

And so they continued on their return journey to Antioch (the one in Syria) from which they had set out, visiting Pamphilia again too, and going back through the mountains to Perge.

Here they stopped and preached for a while and then went on to a port on the coast called Attalia. There they boarded a ship for Antioch and so came back about four years after they had left.

Chapter Seven

The Council of Jerusalem
(Acts 15)

You can imagine how excited the people in Antioch were to see Paul and Barnabas after all that time. And what a rush there was to hear all that had happened to them — where they had been, and what they had done.

Mustn't it have been wonderful to hear them telling about all the countries they had visited and all the new churches they had established, and the adventures they had had? It must have seemed to the people at Antioch that in no time now the whole world would belong to the kingdom of God.

The two Apostles stayed in Antioch for about two years, and then what do you think happened?

Some Christians who had been Pharisees before they were converted came to Antioch and began telling the converts from paganism, "Of course you can't get to Heaven simply by being Christians; you must keep the Law of Moses as well! Everyone in Jerusalem does."

To make it worse still, Peter was in Antioch at that time, and he was so overawed by these grand gentlemen from Jerusalem that he began to refuse to eat with the converts who had been pagans, just as if he didn't know any better.

Poor Peter! This was very silly of him, but I know exactly how he felt, don't you? When people who look extremely wise and respectable are watching you in a disapproving way it *is* awfully difficult to behave as if they weren't there.

Even Barnabas began to behave in the same way; only Paul, a very hard person to overawe, was quite unimpressed. He had realized better than anyone else that it was really true that Jew and Gentile meant nothing any more, but only Christian or not-Christian.

So up stood Paul and told Peter, in front of everyone, what he thought of such behavior. It took courage to do that, you know, because he was well aware that Peter was the head of the Church, the first Pope. But if the Pope does something wrong, he ought to be told so just like anyone else.

We only know about Peter being there from one of Paul's letters, not from Acts; I expect Luke thought it would be unkind to remind everyone what Peter had done, long afterwards when it was all over. He just says that the ex-Pharisees from Jerusalem came to Antioch and began telling the pagan converts they ought to keep the Jewish Law, and that Paul and Barnabas (Barnabas must have seen he was wrong very quickly) had no end of arguments with them.

At last it was decided that Paul and Barnabas and the ex-Pharisees and some of the others who had been most argumentative should all go to Jerusalem and get the matter finally settled by the Apostles there. Peter must have gone to Jerusalem before this, and James, the

The Council of Jerusalem

bishop of Jerusalem, was there, but whether any of the other Apostles were we don't know.

It was about two weeks' journey from Antioch to Jerusalem, and along the way were many places where with little groups of new Christian converts, so the travelers stayed with them and gave them the news about how fast the Church was spreading and about why they were going to Jerusalem. The converts were delighted to have such exciting visitors dropping in on them, and I imagine that they always wanted the visits to last as long as possible — so I think the journey must have taken more than two weeks that time.

But at last they arrived, and all met together at what is called the Council of Jerusalem. All the main people in the Church in Jerusalem were there. Peter, and James the bishop of Jerusalem, and the Jewish converts who had been Pharisees and who wanted the pagan converts to be made to keep the Law of Moses.

Not all converts who had been Pharisees were on their side, of course, after all, Paul himself had been a Pharisee. But most of the people who couldn't bear to let the Old Law go were among them, because Pharisees were especially particular about keeping the Law down to the very last tiny detail.

Luke says that they began with "much disputing." Everyone had something to say, and each one was sure that the point he was going to make would convince everybody else that his side was right.

In fact, you get the idea that they were all getting red in the face and shouting by the time Peter thought everyone had had enough time to give an opinion. Then he stood up, and the rest were quiet at once.

The First Christians

Peter had had plenty of time to think since he had been in Antioch and of course had realized that Paul was quite right, so now he knew exactly what he ought to say.

He began by reminding them all that God had sent him to preach about our Lord to Cornelius, who was a pagan, and that the Holy Spirit had been given to Cornelius and his friends just as He had to the Jewish converts. "God made no difference between them and us," he said, "so how can we? Especially as the Law of Moses has often been too difficult for us or our forefathers to keep. After all it is not by the Law of Moses that we hope to be saved, but by the grace of our Lord Jesus Christ, and so do they."

When the Pope really decides something finally, there is no point in going on arguing about it, and the first Catholics showed that they knew this as well as we do: there was no more argument. But Paul and Barnabas thought that it would help the ex-Pharisees to feel better about it if they told what wonderful things God had done for the pagans they had converted. So each of them made a speech telling about all these things, and you can imagine the people who had hoped the decision would go the other way sitting back and thinking, "Oh, well, I suppose it must be all right," and then as they began to get more used to the idea, "Of course it must be all right. If God no longer makes any difference between Jews and Gentiles, there isn't much point in our trying to."

James, the bishop of Jerusalem, who was our Lord's cousin, had been thinking hard. He was one of the people who had wanted the pagans to keep the Jewish Law,

The Council of Jerusalem

but now he could see he had been wrong, and when Paul and Barnabas had finished speaking, he said that now he had something to say.

What he said was that Peter had told them how God had chosen a people for Himself from among the Gentiles, and that there was really no reason to be so surprised about it. The prophets had said it would happen: God had always meant to call the Gentiles to Himself at last.

Then he made a good suggestion: that a letter should be written and sent round to all the churches where there were converts from paganism, telling them they need not keep the Jewish Law, but asking them to avoid two things for the sake of not upsetting their Jewish-Christian neighbors, and reminding them not to do something else which was a sin.

The things they were to avoid were eating meat from animals that had been offered in sacrifice to idols, or from animals that had been killed by strangling or any other sort of meat that had blood in it; the third thing was quite different, a sin against purity called fornication. Why those three things particularly?

Meat that had been offered to pagan idols was sold in the market like any other meat. The pagan converts had bought it all their lives and thought nothing of it, but the Jewish converts wouldn't have dreamed of buying it. Meat from animals killed by strangling had blood in it and that, or any meat with blood in it, had always been forbidden to the Jews; they couldn't bear the idea of eating it. And, as I expect you know, even nowadays, the Jewish religion forbids it, and that is what it means when you see meat in a butcher's marked "Kosher":

there's no blood in it, and it is all right for the strictest Jew to eat.

Now, in the Apostles' days Mass was usually in the evening, and before it the people who were going to Mass met together for supper. It was rather the same idea as a Communion breakfast, only there were no rules about fasting before Holy Communion then, so they had the meal beforehand.

Well, suppose you went to a Communion breakfast in someone's house, and your hostess came in smiling brightly and put a roast puppy on the table to be carved? I think you would find it difficult to be polite about it and it might very well put you off Communion breakfasts altogether!

The Jews felt just like that about meat offered to idols and from strangled animals, so you see how sensible James was to ask the pagan converts to give it up.

The third thing they were told not to do was quite a different matter. The pagan converts, who did not have Ten Commandments to keep them straight nor the prophets to pull them up when they started to go wrong, had really got rather mixed up about what was a sin and what wasn't. Fornication is a sin against purity that they had forgotten was a sin, so they needed to be reminded that it was, and that they mustn't do it.

James finished up his speech by saying (to comfort the Pharisee converts, I suppose) that after all Moses' words were read every week in all the synagogues all over the world, so there was no chance of his being forgotten.

When the letter was written, it was sent with Paul and Barnabas and Judas and Silas to the church at

The Council of Jerusalem

Antioch, and to the churches in Syria and Cilicia, telling them what the Council had decided. You can read the whole letter in the fifteenth chapter of the Acts of the Apostles, and I hope you will. It is the sort of letter you can imagine the Pope sending now, but not anybody else.

When Paul and Barnabas, Judas and Silas arrived in Antioch with the letter telling the pagan converts that it was quite settled they need not keep the Jewish Law, and telling them the few things they must do, everybody was delighted — there was, Luke says, "much rejoicing." It was wonderful to know just where they stood and what they were to do, and to be quite sure they need not listen to anyone who told them anything different.

Judas and Silas encouraged them also and, I am sure, told them all about the Council of Jerusalem. After they stayed in Antioch for a while, Judas decided it was time for him to go back to Jerusalem, but Silas thought he would stay on in Antioch.

After a time, Paul said to Barnabas, "Let's go back and visit all the new churches we started and see how they are getting on."

Barnabas agreed and said, "And we will take Mark with us."

Mark, the man who wrote one of the Gospels, had started out with them before on their first journey, but he turned around and went home when they got to Pamphilia.

Barnabas, who must have known Mark better than Paul, wanted to give him a second chance, but Paul wouldn't have it.

The First Christians

"No," he said, "he came with us before, and look what happened — he went home before we had really got started. I won't have him."

They disagreed so violently that in the end Barnabas took Mark and went off to Cyprus, and Paul took Silas instead of Barnabas on his second great journey.

So you see once more, even saints can disagree. I am rather sorry for poor Mark, he must have been so embarrassed at these two great men quarreling over him.

The rest of the Acts of the Apostles tell us more about Mark (Barnabas was quite right about him, of course) but no more about Barnabas. But I can tell you what happened to him — he was martyred in Cyprus, and so far as we know he and Paul didn't meet again until they met in Heaven.

Chapter Eight

The Second Great Journey Begins
(Acts 15 cont., 16, 17)

Paul and Silas began their journey by traveling all through Syria and Cilicia and visiting the churches there, stopping a little while with each to see that they were remembering everything Paul had taught them, to confirm new converts, and to encourage them all to go on being good and faithful Christians.

When they had finished there, they went to visit the churches at Derbe and Lystra, to see how Paul's converts there were getting on.

In one of these cities they made friends with a young Christian man called Timothy. His mother was one of Paul's Jewish converts and his father was a Christian who had been born a pagan. Paul and Silas must have liked Timothy very much as soon as they met him, because they decided to take him along on their travels.

Timothy had never been circumcised because of his father being a pagan, so Paul circumcised him before they set off on their journey again. It was all very well to insist that converts from paganism need not keep the Jewish Law, but quite another matter to upset the Jews

The First Christians

they would meet in their travels when it could so easily be avoided. The Jewish Christians they met were sure to ask Timothy if he had been circumcised, as soon as they heard that he had a Jewish mother, and to be scandalized if it had not been done, just as we would be dismayed to find that a boy who had a Jewish father and a Catholic mother had never been baptized.

When it was done, the three of them — Paul, Silas, and Timothy — set out, going from city to city, visiting all the new churches Paul and Barnabas had founded on their journey; encouraging them and telling them about the Council of Jerusalem and what had been decided there. Everywhere they found the Church flourishing with new converts coming in every day.

They traveled on through Phrygia and Galatia, and just which way they went is something that scholars still argue about. I am certainly not going to get into the argument, so I shall only say that whichever way it was, they intended to go and preach in the part of Turkey which used to be called Asia, but the Holy Spirit let Paul know that they were not to preach there.

So then they thought of going to a place called Bithynia, but the Holy Spirit said they were not to preach there either.

It wasn't because these places were not to hear about our Lord, they did hear about Him soon afterwards, but just now Paul and his companions were to go somewhere else where they were badly needed.

If you look at a map of Turkey you will see that it comes to a sort of point at the northwest corner. Here was a port called Troas, and to this port Paul and his companions came, still not sure where they were to go.

The Second Great Journey Begins

But at Troas Paul had a vision of a man of Macedonia, which was just across the water to the north. In his vision the man stood beside him and pleaded with him saying, "Come over to Macedonia and help us!"

And do you know who some people think the man in the vision was? Luke himself! No one can be sure about it, but it would be just like Luke to say Paul had this vision and not say, "And I was the man he saw."

Luke arrived in Troas just after Paul had seen the vision. We know that for certain because he starts saying "we" did this and that to show he was there instead of saying "they" did this and that.

All of them were now certain that they were to go to Macedonia, so they took the first ship they could find and sailed off for Neapolis, which was a Macedonian port. From there they went a few miles inland to Philippi, the chief city of that part of Macedonia.

If you look at the map, you will see where it is — a long thin piece of land between Bulgaria and the Aegean Sea. You will see something else, too: Paul and his friends were now, for the first time, in Europe, so Philippi was the first place in Europe to hear about our Lord.

Here they stayed for some days, talking about all sorts of things, planning where they would preach, no doubt, and, I think, talking about something else as well: the Gospel that Luke was to write, or perhaps had already begun to write.

Philippi was a Roman colony and there were not many Jews there, and no synagogue, but Paul heard that on the Sabbath some of the Jewish women met for prayers at a pleasant place beside a river. So they went

The First Christians

out to this place and found the group of women. After the prayers were done they sat down to tell them about our Lord.

One of the women there was not Jewish, she had been brought up a pagan, but had learnt to believe in the true God, and went to pray with the Jewish women. Her name was Lydia, and she seems to have been fairly wealthy: her trade was selling purple cloth which was made and dyed in the place she came from — Thyatira.

God put it into her mind to listen carefully to Paul, and she believed all he was saying, and was his first convert in Europe.

All her household came into the Church with her, and after they were baptized she said to Paul, "Now that I belong to the true Church, you and your friends must come and stay with me in my house, instead of living in lodgings."

When Paul and the others said that really she need not do that, and that four guests all at once would be too much and so on, she just wouldn't take no for an answer, and so they did all go and stay with her and they made her house the center of their missionary work. I like Lydia very much — I wonder if anyone who is reading this is named Lydia.

Paul and his friends went on going to the place by the river for prayers, both to pray themselves and to preach and make more converts.

One day as they were going toward it they met a slave girl who was, says Luke, "possessed by a divining spirit." A devil had taken possession of her and through her he told people's fortunes (and plenty of lies, I don't doubt). The people who owned her made a great deal of

The Second Great Journey Begins

money out of this fortune telling and considered her and her devil very valuable property.

Well, when she saw Paul and Silas she turned and followed them crying out aloud, "These men are servants of the most High God, preaching to us the way to be saved!"

Whether God had forced the devil to do this, or whether the girl managed to do it herself in spite of him, we can't really know, but anyway that is what happened, not only the first time she saw Paul and his companions, but every time she saw them afterwards.

At last Paul was so sorry for her, he turned around and said to the devil, "I command you to come out of her in the name of our Lord Jesus Christ."

The devil left her there and then, and I'm sure the girl was very glad to be rid of him. But when the men who owned the slave girl found out that she was no longer able to tell fortunes they were simply furious. So what do you think her owners did then?

They had Paul and Silas arrested, bringing them before the magistrates and claiming, "These Jews are disturbing the peace.

The First Christians

They are recommending customs that are not fit for Roman citizens."

Philippi was a Roman colony that was very proud of its Roman-ness. There were only a few Jews there and they seem to have been unpopular: probably because they were not exactly like everybody else, which is one of the silliest possible reasons for not liking people, and one of the ones you meet most often.

Anyway, a crowd gathered and began to shout whatever they heard these men saying and to make a great deal of noise, as bad-tempered crowds will. The magistrates, who don't seem to have been very good ones, were frightened by all this and told their officers to pull the prisoners' clothes off and beat them.

This was flat against Roman law: Paul and Silas had only been accused, not judged, and anyway they were Roman citizens, so no one had a right to beat them. But they were terribly beaten all the same, and then thrown into prison, and the jailer was told to be sure and keep them secure. He put them in the inner part of the prison with their feet fastened through holes in planks of wood. This was very uncomfortable for the prisoners, but certainly seemed secure. No doubt it would have kept in ordinary prisoners, but not prisoners which God wanted set free.

In the middle of the night as Paul and Silas were cheerfully saying their prayers, there was a terrible earthquake. The ground under the prison shook so much that all the doors flew open and the prisoners' chains came undone.

The jailer jumped out of bed and rushed to the prison. When he saw the prison doors open, he drew his

The Second Great Journey Begins

sword, meaning to kill himself, for he knew he would be killed anyway if the prisoners were gone.

But Paul saw him and shouted at the top of his voice, "Do not hurt yourself! We are all here!"

So the jailer put back his sword, called for a light, and came running into the prison in a great state of mind.

You know, I think he had suspected all along that Paul and Silas were preaching the truth and knew the way to Heaven, and now that God had sent this earthquake to free them, he was sure of it. So he fell down at their feet, shaking all over, and said, "Sirs, what am I to do to save myself?"

He meant "to save myself from being killed," but Paul told him about a more important way of being saved.

"Have faith," said Paul, "in the Lord Jesus: that is the way for you to be saved and for all your household, too."

By this time, you may be sure, everyone from the jailer's house was there, wondering what on earth was going on. And Paul stood in the entrance hall of the prison and told them about our Lord and His Church.

Then the jailer took him and Silas to his own house and washed their poor sore backs and gave them breakfast, and he and all his house were very happy indeed and were all baptized that same night.

In the morning, the magistrates, who had probably decided that they had been a bit hasty the day before, sent word to the jailer that Paul and Silas were to be allowed to go free. The jailer was delighted. "Now you can go home," he said. "Everything is all right!"

The First Christians

But Paul didn't agree. "What?" he said. "They beat Roman citizens in public, when they haven't even been judged, and then say 'they can go home'! That will not do at all. They must come themselves and let us out."

When this message was taken to the magistrates, they were very frightened because they hadn't understood before that Paul and Silas were not just stray Jews, but Jews who were Roman citizens. So they came to the prison and asked them very politely please to come out, and said that the whole thing was a most unfortunate mistake, and so on, and that they would be so grateful if Paul and Silas would please not report them, and if it was quite convenient, would they leave the city soon, in case of any more trouble?

That was more like it. So Paul and Silas kindly agreed to come out of prison and leave the city, but first they went back to Lydia's house and told the people there all about it, and cheered them up, and I expect made them laugh, too, over the sudden politeness of the magistrates.

After Paul and Silas left Lydia's house they journeyed farther along the coast, still going west. The first city they came to was called Amphipolis, and the second Apollonia, but they did not stay to preach in either of these places. They pressed on to Thessalonica, the most important city in that part of the world, and a great port, with all sorts of ships busily coming and going in its harbor. Thessalonica has not disappeared, like so many of the cities of those days, it even has almost the same name now as it had then — Salonika.

Here Paul and Silas lodged with a Jewish man called Jason. Luke doesn't say whether he was an old friend of

The Second Great Journey Begins

Paul's, or whether Paul converted him after they met in this city. But whether he was a Christian when Paul and Silas arrived or not, we know he was one soon afterwards and his house was the headquarters for the new Church beginning in Thessalonica.

For the first three weeks of their stay in this city, Paul and Silas went to the synagogue and preached to the Jews about our Lord.

Besides the Jews themselves, there were always people there who had been brought up to be pagans, but who had learned from the Jews to believe in the true God. Lydia was one of such people in Philippi, you remember. A great number of these believed Paul and Silas and joined the Church, and so did some of the Jews themselves. But the remaining Jews were terribly jealous at seeing how much influence Paul had, and how readily everyone seemed to follow him. We do not know how long he stayed in Thessalonica, but at last these Jews felt they could bear it no longer. So they hired a lot of the sort of men you can find in any city who are always ready to do almost anything for a price, and got them to start a riot against the Christians.

When the city was in an uproar, they attacked Jason's house, meaning to drag Paul and Silas out, but they couldn't find them. So they took Jason and some of the other Christians who happened to be there, and brought them to the city council and began accusing *them* of having started all the trouble!

"Here they are!" they said. "These are the men who are turning everything upside down! And this is Jason, whose house they use. All these people defy Caesar — they say there is another king, called Jesus."

The First Christians

The city council was alarmed when they heard this, and so were the crowd who had gathered to see what happened. Were these men who had been living in their city traitors? But the city council didn't lose their heads. They let Jason and the other Christians out on bail, which probably annoyed their accusers, especially as the two people they wanted to catch most were still free. The Christians were determined that these two, Paul and Silas, were going to stay free, too, so under cover of darkness they got them out of the city, and safely away. Beroea was the place they sent them to, a city about fifty miles southwest of Thessalonica.

When they arrived they went straight to the synagogue. Here they found the best Jews they had found anywhere. When Paul and Silas quoted texts from the Old Testament to them which showed that our Lord was the Christ whose coming had been foretold by so many prophets, they went and looked the texts up, and really studied as hard as they could every day, to see if Paul and Silas were right.

A great many of them were converted and so were numbers of pagans — in fact, Beroea was a tremendous success for Paul and Silas, and they stayed there for some time getting the new little church on its feet.

But presently the Jews in Thessalonica heard what was happening in Beroea. Of course they were furious and they sent men down to try and start trouble there, too.

When the Beroean Christians found out what was happening they sent Paul away to continue his journey along the coast by himself, but Silas and Timothy stayed where they were for the time being.

The Second Great Journey Begins

I think Paul, even if he was, as they say, an ugly man, must have been a person you would always know again if you had once seen him. And he was quite without fear, so that you couldn't tell what he would do in any situation, however alarming. Anyway, once trouble threatened anywhere, everyone's idea seems to have been to get Paul away as quickly as possible.

Chapter Nine

Paul Goes On Alone
(Acts 17 cont., 18, 19)

Some of the new Beroean Christians went with Paul as far as Athens and then came back to Beroea. Paul sent a message by them to say he would like Silas and Timothy to join him there as soon as they could.

In Athens, Paul was so struck to find the whole city full of idols that he couldn't keep to his usual plan of preaching only in the synagogue to start with. He did that, but he also stood up in the marketplace and talked to, and argued with, anyone who would listen.

And there were plenty of people willing to listen, for the people of Athens loved nothing so much as a chance to hear or tell something new.

We need not feel too superior about it either — we are all rather like that ourselves! Anyhow, the Athenians were very pleased to listen to Paul and to talk to him, but doing anything about what he said was quite another matter.

There were a great many people in Athens in those days who thought idols were rather silly, and who were very busy trying to make up a good religion out of their own heads. It had to be a religion for this world because

The First Christians

none of them really believed in another. These people were called philosophers, and there were several different kinds of them, but none of them believed in a life after this one or in the true God. If you know as little as that, you aren't going to be very good at planning how to live even in this world. But at least men like these listened to Paul and found what he said very new indeed and so worth hearing.

The highest law court in Athens was called the Areopagus, and it was a very grand and special sort of law court. The people who belonged to it were called Areopagites (I'm sorry about these odd names, but I didn't invent them). They had to be over sixty years old and from the grandest families, so I don't suppose there were many of them, and I am quite sure they had a very high opinion of themselves.

Well, some of the philosophers who met Paul in the marketplace thought it would be fun to take him and introduce him to these Areopagites and see what they would make of him. So they took him up to the Areopagus (it was quite nearby) and the old gentlemen there asked him very politely to please tell them what in the world he was talking about.

Now Paul had noticed an altar in Athens that was dedicated to the "Unknown God." This had been built in remembrance of some odd and remarkable thing that had happened on that spot, something that the Athenians thought one of the gods must be responsible for, but as they had no idea which, they called him "the unknown god."

Paul knew that was all it meant, but he thought the inscription was truer than the people who wrote it

Paul Goes On Alone

knew — there was a God who was quite unknown to them: the true God. So he used this idea in his sermon.

This is what he said, "Men of Athens, wherever I look I see how religious you are. Why, you even have an altar, among all the rest, dedicated to the Unknown God. Now this is just the God I can tell you about! He is the God who made heaven and earth. He doesn't live in temples built by men — He doesn't need us to make temples, or anything else, for Him for it is He who gives us our lives and everything we have. He made all mankind, leaving each nation to search for Him, to see if they could find their way to Him. But all the same, He is not far away — we live and move in Him — and as some of your own poets have told us, 'We are His children.'

"But if we are children of God, how are we to suppose that He can be like these idols, made of gold or silver or stone carved by artists? These are just foolish things. Now, at last, this true God is calling on all men everywhere to repent because the day is coming on which He will judge the whole world.

"And the Man who told us this He has shown to be true, by raising Him up from death."

This was too much for many of them to believe — a man coming to life again after he had died! Some of them mocked Paul, others said politely, "Well, you must tell us more about this — some other time."

Only a few of them went with Paul to hear more and came to believe in our Lord. One of them was a man named Dionysius, which we call Denis in English, who was one of the Areopagites themselves, and another was a girl called Damaris.

The First Christians

Dionysius is said to have been the first bishop of Athens. We don't know what happened to Damaris, but I would like to. I always wonder why so many boys are called Denis after Dionysius, but so few girls are called after Damaris. It's such a pretty name.

After this, Paul decided Athens was too ready to listen but too slow to believe and he left it even before Silas and Timothy arrived, and went on to Corinth.

If you would like to read the whole of Paul's speech before the Areopagites, you will find it in the seventeenth chapter of Acts.

From Athens, Paul sailed away over the sea, still going west, and so came to Corinth. The port he landed at was called Cenchrae, just a few miles from the city. Corinth was built on a narrow neck of land between two great ports, and a terrific amount of trade going east and west across the world went by way of this city. This made it a very important place indeed, and it was full of people busily engaged in getting as rich as they possibly could as fast as they possibly could.

Here Paul met a married couple who were Christian Jews from Rome, called Aquila and Priscilla. They had come to Corinth because all Jewish people, whether they were Christian or not, had been turned out of Rome as "troublemakers."

Luke doesn't tell us why, but another man who wrote history, a pagan, says it was because they were always making trouble on account of somebody called "Chrestus."

It sounds as if Christians in Rome had been having just the same kind of trouble with the Jews as Paul had in so many other places, doesn't it? Anyway, the

Paul Goes On Alone

Romans were tired of the whole thing, so they had turned them all out to make an end of it.

Paul made friends with Aquila and Priscilla at once and as Aquila, like Paul, was a tentmaker by trade, he settled down in Aquila's house and they worked at making tents together.

Every week Paul went to the synagogue and told the Jews about our Lord, but they wouldn't listen and talked blasphemy. Meantime, Silas and Timothy, whom Paul had left in Beroea, finally caught up with him, and you can imagine how delighted he was to see them again.

When he was sure it was no use preaching in the synagogue any more, he told the Jews plainly that they had had their chance and now he was going to preach to the pagans.

Next door to the synagogue was a house belonging to a man called Titus Justus, who had learned to believe in God, and it was in this house that Paul started the first Christian church in Corinth. That was just like Paul, wasn't it? But Crispus, the head of the synagogue, was converted after all, and so were all his family, and many of the pagans began to come in as converts too.

So, Paul, who had been feeling rather sad ever since he had had so little success in Athens, began to feel better. But I expect he wasn't sure whether God wanted him to stay in Corinth or whether he ought to go somewhere else, because our Lord came to him in a vision. "Do not be afraid," our Lord said, "speak out, and refuse to be quiet, I am with you. There are a great many people in this city who belong to me."

So then Paul cheered up completely and settled down to build up a strong church in Corinth.

The First Christians

Everything went well and more and more converts came in. It was a whole year and a half before trouble started. The Jews had a new leader at their synagogue called Sosthenes, instead of Crispus, and he and his congregation didn't like Paul and the Christians next door any better as time went on. They waited patiently for a chance to get rid of them.

When a new Roman proconsul called Gallio was put in charge of Corinth, they thought the moment had come. "He won't know the ropes when he first arrives," they said to each other, "so now is the moment to make trouble for the Christians."

They pounced on Paul and brought him before Gallio's judgment seat, saying, "This fellow is persuading people to worship in a way our Law forbids."

Paul was just opening his mouth to defend himself, when Gallio, who was no fool, even if he was new to his job, said, "If you Jews were accusing this man of a crime, it would be right for me to listen to you patiently, but as it is only a matter of your own Law — words and names and so on — you had better see to it yourselves. It is no business of mine."

And with that he had them all turned out.

Now the Jews were not much liked at Corinth for some reason, so the rest of the people, seeing him snubbed by Gallio, set upon Sosthenes and beat him. Gallio could see what was going on, but he paid no attention at all. So that was one time the unbelieving Jews' persecution of the Christians rather backfired, wasn't it?

Paul stayed on in Corinth for some time after this, but at last he said good-bye to the Christians there and

Paul Goes On Alone

sailed off to Syria. Before he left he made a vow to go to Jerusalem, and as a sign of his vow he shaved his head.

This was the Jewish custom, but if tradition is right and Paul was rather bald anyway, I daresay it didn't make much difference to him. However, he shaved off whatever hair he could find.

Priscilla and Aquila went with Paul as far as Ephesus, a port city in what we call Turkey, which was on his way.

Here he preached in the synagogue once. The Jews there asked him to stay; they wanted to hear more, but he said no, he must go on to Jerusalem, but he would come back to them afterwards if it was God's will.

In the meantime, he left Aquila and Priscilla in Ephesus while he himself went on to Caesarea by sea, and from there to Jerusalem.

If you are reading Acts, you might miss his visit altogether, and wonder what happened to his vow. Luke only says "he went up and greeted the Church." But people who are learned about such things agree that "the Church" Paul went to pay his respects to was the mother Church at Jerusalem.

After this he went to Antioch again to see how they were getting on there and he stayed there for some time — even Paul had to have a rest once in a while.

The First Christians

When he was ready, he set off again and once more visited the churches in Galatia and Phrygia.

In the meantime, Aquila and Priscilla were still in Ephesus when a visitor from Alexandria arrived. He was a Jew called Apollo. They were very much interested in him because he spoke about our Lord in the synagogue and out of it, and seemed to know the Old Testament very well. But as they listened to him they discovered that there was a lot he didn't know: for instance, he had never heard of any kind of baptism, except John the Baptist's kind. So they thought it would be a good idea to make friends with him, and they did, and found him very willing to learn all the parts of the faith he had not heard of yet.

Apollo was on his way to Achaia, so the Christians in Ephesus gave him letters to the Christians there, and they were very glad to see him indeed. He knew the Scriptures so well and was such a good speaker that he was delighted to prove to the Jews that our Lord was the Christ as often as ever they would listen.

It was after Apollo had left Ephesus that Paul finished his journey through Phrygia and Galatia and came back there. Paul, you remember, had promised the Jews that he would come back and tell them more about our Lord, if God would let him. On his way to the synagogue he met a dozen or so Christians and of course he stopped to talk to them.

After they had been talking for a while Paul said to them, "Was the Holy Spirit given to you when you learned to believe?"

He meant, "Have you been confirmed?" But he got a surprise. These Christians didn't know what he was

Paul Goes On Alone

talking about. "We haven't heard anything about a Holy Spirit," they said.

"Well!" said Paul. "But what sort of baptism did you receive?" And then it was all explained: "John's baptism," they said.

Perhaps they had been taught about our Lord by Apollo before Aquila and Priscilla made friends with him, or perhaps some other follower of John the Baptist had taught them.

Anyway, Paul told them now that John's baptism was only a sign of repentance and reminded them that John had said there was someone who would come after him who was much more important than he was. Paul told them that this was Jesus and explained some more to them, and then they were baptized properly and confirmed.

As soon as Paul confirmed them, the Holy Spirit came down on them and they found they could speak languages they had not learned and they could prophesy. So then they knew all about the Holy Spirit, and I am sure that they were very glad they had met Paul.

I do wish things like that happened now when we are confirmed, but still we receive the Holy Spirit just as they did — even if it doesn't show — and that is the most important thing after all.

After this Paul went to the synagogue and taught there for three months. By the end of that time he felt sure all those who were going to believe him had been converted, and as the others were getting more and more bad-tempered and unwilling to listen, he thought it was time to find somewhere else to take his converts while they were learning to be Christians.

The First Christians

There was a man called Tyrannus in Ephesus who ran a school and Paul asked him if he and his Christians could use it out of school hours. Tyrannus said, "Yes," and this plan worked beautifully: the Christians met in this school for two whole years.

Luke says everything went so well that not only Ephesus but the whole of the part of Turkey which was called Asia heard about our Lord, both Jews and pagans alike.

God did a great number of miracles through Paul while he was in Ephesus, far more than were usual even in those days. The aprons he wore when he was making tents, and even his handkerchiefs, used to be taken to touch anyone who was ill or troubled by the devil, and the sick man would get well, or the devil would go away, as soon as the handkerchief or apron touched him.

I wonder if Paul knew where all his aprons and handkerchiefs were disappearing to, or if the people who took them always remembered to bring them back.

There were some Jews in Ephesus at that time who went about casting out devils, or trying to, by magic. They saw that Paul was much better at casting out devils than they were, so they thought they would try doing it as he did.

The next time a man possessed by the devil was brought to them they ordered the devil to go, "In the name of Jesus who is preached by Paul." But the devil answered, "Jesus I know, and Paul I know, *but who are you?*" And with that the possessed man pounced on them and attacked them and got the better of them, so that they ran away as hard as they could go, wounded and with their clothes torn off.

Paul Goes On Alone

Everyone in Ephesus heard about this and they were very frightened indeed. Christians who had anything on their consciences came to confession in a hurry and a lot of people who had been trying to practice magic decided that it wasn't safe if this sort of thing could happen, so they brought their magic-making books and made an enormous bonfire of them. These books were worth a great deal of money, too, so you can tell they meant it.

Chapter Ten

The Riot in Ephesus
(Acts 19 cont., 20, 21)

Paul had been two years in Ephesus: the Church was large there, and all was going well. Presently he thought he would go to Jerusalem again and on his way collect some money for the poor in Jerusalem from the Christians in Macedonia and Achaia who were better off.

Paul sent Timothy and another friend of his called Erastus ahead of him: they were to take up the collection and Paul was to follow them in a few days. Luke doesn't say why — perhaps a friend of his was getting married and he wanted to stay for the wedding or something of that sort.

The greatest pagan temple in the whole world was at Ephesus. It was very large and very grand indeed and it was dedicated to a goddess called Diana of Ephesus. This was not the rather nice Diana you sometimes read about in the Greek myths, but quite a different one.

Her other name was Cybele and she was really a most unpleasant sort of goddess. But the pagan people were very proud of her and of having this wonderful shrine in her honor in Ephesus. People used to come there on pilgrimage from all over the place, as we go to

The First Christians

Lourdes or Rome, and, just like us, they wanted to take something home to show their friends when they got back. As we buy a rosary or a medal, so they used to buy a little model of the shrine — a tiny temple of Diana made of silver.

A great many people made their living, and even got quite rich, by making and selling these little silver shrines. This made Ephesus great place for silversmiths. One of the most important of these silversmiths was called Demetrius, and he had been noticing for some time that Christians were just as bad as Jews from his point of view — they never bought models of Diana's shrine! And there were so many Christians by this time, both in Ephesus and in the country around it, that trade was getting bad.

So Demetrius called a meeting of all the silversmiths and said to them, "Friends, you know that our trade depends on the sale of these models of Diana's temple. But this Paul has persuaded thousands of people to worship some other god instead of her, and he tells them that idols made by men are not gods at all. If this goes on we shall have no trade left. And not only that, but our great temple of Diana will be deserted and the goddess herself will be forgotten — this great goddess who is worshipped by all the world!"

When the silversmiths heard this story they were furious and began to shout, "Great is Diana of Ephesus!"

They made such a noise that soon the whole city was in an uproar. In Ephesus there was a very large outdoor theater, even bigger than Madison Square Garden in New York or Olympia in London, that could hold twenty-five thousand people.

The Riot in Ephesus

Presently all these silversmiths ran to this theater to hold a bigger and better meeting there. On their way, they caught two of Paul's companions from Macedonia, called Gaius and Aristarchus, and forced them to come to the theater, too. All sorts of other people joined them on their way, just for the fun of going with all these shouting people, and they all crowded into the theater, making more noise than ever.

When Paul heard all this excitement and discovered what it was about, he was all for going to the theater himself to talk to them, which was just like Paul.

But the other Christians wouldn't let him, and while he was still arguing about it some of the Greek officials in charge of the arrangements for entertainments and feast days sent messages to him saying the same thing — that he was on no account to risk his life by going to the theater.

So he gave in and stayed at home.

Meanwhile, the row in the theater went on, full strength, everybody shouting at the tops of their voices, especially the ones who had no idea what it was all about!

The Jews of Ephesus were very much afraid that at any moment the silversmiths would remember again that they didn't buy silver shrines any more than the Christians, so they pushed a man called Alexander forward to speak to the crowd, in the hope that he might be able to calm them down.

In the crush, he was carried right up to the front of the theater and there he stood up and waved his hands for silence, so that he could speak. The crowd quieted enough to let him begin, but as soon as they heard his

The First Christians

voice they knew he was a Jew (I suppose he spoke Greek with an accent) and they all began yelling again, "Great is Diana of Ephesus."

And do you know they kept that up for two whole hours. It must have been very hard on their throats, and I should think a lot of them were quite glad when at long last the town clerk turned up. A town clerk was something like the mayor in our cities, and he was a Greek official, not a Roman. He was a very sensible town clerk, though goodness knows why he took such ages to turn up. Anyway when he did arrive, everyone was ready to be quiet and listen to him.

"Isn't all this rather silly?" he said. "As if everybody didn't know that the whole city of Ephesus is the guardian of the great shrine of Diana and of the image of her which came to us from the sky. No one has said anything against her and you had much better be quiet and do nothing rash. You have brought these men here by force," — he meant Gaius and Aristarchus — "but they have not robbed the temple, they have said nothing against your goddess. If Demetrius and his fellow craftsmen have anything against them, why do they not go to the law? If there is anything the matter, let it be settled in a law-abiding way. There may very well be trouble with the Romans over this day's doings as it is, and what are we to answer when they ask why there was a riot? We shall have nothing to say." With that he told them to go home, and so they did, feeling rather foolish, too, I daresay.

After it was all over, Paul called a meeting of his own. He wanted to cheer his Christians up and encourage them and also to say good-bye, because he was ready

The Riot in Ephesus

by then to start out for Jerusalem, though he was in no great hurry to get there and meant to go through Macedonia first, encouraging all the little and big churches as he came to them. He did that and then went on into Greece, meaning to get a ship from Corinth to Syria. But he heard that the Jews in Greece were making a plot against him. There were a lot of them waiting to sail to Jerusalem, as he was, to keep the Pasch there, and they meant to murder him on the voyage. This didn't appeal to Paul much, so he went back through Macedonia to Philippi. Some of his companions who were going with him went on ahead. They crossed the Aegean sea and waited for him at Troas, the port on the northwest tip of Turkey.

Paul stayed in Philippi over the Pasch. This, as you know, was the feast the Jews kept every year to remember the way God had brought them out of slavery in Egypt. (You can find a really exciting account of it in the twelfth chapter of the book of Exodus in the Old Testament.) What they didn't know, of course, was that the lamb they killed for the Paschal feast was only a sort of promise of our Lord, who, when He came, died for the whole world. That's why He is called the Lamb of God, and why He died at Paschal time.

Well, when the feast days were over, Paul sailed off to Troas to join his friends. And who do you think went with him? Luke! He turns up in the story again at this point, and I am very glad to find him there.

What do you think he had been doing since he last saw Paul? Nobody knows for sure, but I think it is a good guess that he had been to Jerusalem to ask our Lady and the other people there about our Lord, so that

The First Christians

he could write his Gospel. By now I imagine he had written part of it and wanted to show Paul.

However that may be, he and Paul crossed the sea together and met Paul's companions at Troas, and stayed there a week. The last day they were there was a Saturday, which, for the Jews, of course, was like Sunday is for us. But they had a way of counting days that seems very odd: as soon as darkness fell in the evening it counted as the beginning of the next day. So after dark on Saturday counted as the beginning of Sunday.

The Christians who had been brought up as Jews still kept Saturday for rest and prayer, and when the day was over, on what we would call Saturday evening but they called the beginning of Sunday, they met for supper and Mass.

Paul preached to them on this, his last evening in Troas. He had a great deal to tell them — so much that he was still speaking at midnight.

Don't be too surprised. Remember that it may have been quite late at night when he began. Still, what with the lateness and the room being very hot because there were a lot of lamps burning in it, one of his congregation, at least, fell fast asleep.

The Riot in Ephesus

This was a boy called Eutychus — which means "good luck" — but he had bad luck. He was sitting on the windowsill, so naturally when he went to sleep he fell out of the window.

The room they were in was on the fourth floor of the house and when everyone rushed down they found Eutychus lying on the ground, quite dead.

Paul came down with the rest and bent over the boy and put his arms around him. Then he said, "There is no need to worry: he is alive."

It didn't look like it, but they supposed Paul knew, so they all went back upstairs and Paul said Mass and gave them Holy Communion. Afterwards, he and the rest sat talking, waiting until it was light enough to travel. Then he left them, and as everybody got their belongings together to leave, they found that Paul had been quite right about Eutychus: he woke up perfectly well, which was a great comfort to everybody. So he did have good luck after all.

The reason Paul set off alone was that he wanted to walk and the rest were going on to the next port by ship. The port was Assos, just across the northwest point of Turkey. It was thirty miles away by land, and why in the world Paul wanted to walk there after being up all night, when he could just as well have gone by ship, I can't imagine. But that is what he did, and I think it is rather astonishing that he wanted to.

At Assos, Paul got on board the ship and they all sailed away down the coast of Turkey to Mitylene. From there they went on farther down the coast, past Ephesus to Miletus. Paul didn't want to go to Ephesus itself, because he was in a hurry to get to Jerusalem in time for

The First Christians

Pentecost and he knew that there would be too many people who wanted to see him in Ephesus and too many invitations to dinner that it would be difficult to refuse. But he did want to see his special friends, the priests he had left in charge at Ephesus, so he sent a message to them from Miletus, asking them to come and see him there.

When they arrived, he made a speech to them. This is what he said, "You know how I have lived among you since the first day I set foot in your part of the country, serving the Lord humbly, and not without weeping over the trials I met through the plotting of the Jews. I never failed you, did I? I preached and taught you both publicly and in your own houses. I have told both Jews and Greeks that they must repent before God and have faith in our Lord Jesus Christ.

"Now I am going to Jerusalem and what will happen to me there I do not know. I only know that in every city the Holy Spirit tells me that imprisonment and sorrow are waiting for me there. I don't mind that, my work is more important than I am: I must run the course God has set me and finish my task of preaching which the Lord Jesus has given me, proclaiming the good news of His grace. Here I am then, to say good-bye to you. I know very well that you, among whom I have lived so long, preaching to you the kingdom of God, will never see my face again. So I ask you to be witnesses that if any of your souls are lost, it is not my fault: I never feared to reveal God's whole plan to you. Keep watch then, over yourselves, and over God's Church, in which the Holy Spirit has made you bishops. You are to be shepherds of that flock which He won for Himself at

The Riot in Ephesus

the price of His own blood. I know very well that wolves will come and attack the flock, men of your own, who will preach false doctrine and who will find people ready to believe them. Be on the watch then, do not forget all that I have told you in the three years I have spent among you. Now, as always, I commend you to God who can build you up and give you your own place among the saints.

"I never asked for silver or gold or clothing from any man: you know that. You know how I have worked with these hands of mine and have provided all that I and my companions needed. Always I have tried to show you that it is our duty to work hard to support the weak. Remember how our Lord said: 'It is more blessed to give than to receive.' "

When he had finished speaking he knelt down and prayed with them all. They were desperately sad and could hardly say good-bye for crying, especially because he said that they would never see his face again. And no wonder — it nearly makes me cry now, just to read what he said. You can read his words, much more completely than I have given them here, in the twentieth chapter of the Acts of the Apostles. The odd thing is, that they probably did see Paul again, after all. The Holy Spirit had not told him he was to be a martyr in Jerusalem, only that he was to be imprisoned there: he must have thought this could only lead to his death, but he was wrong, as you will see.

That saying of our Lord's, "It is more blessed to give than to receive," is not in any of the Gospels, so if Paul had not quoted it, and Luke had not been there to write it down, we would never have heard of it at all.

The First Christians

Paul left Miletus after he had said good-bye to the bishops and priests from Ephesus. (Luke says, "We tore ourselves away from them.") He and his companions boarded their ship and sailed off, touching at various ports, but not staying anywhere until they came to Tyre.

This was the capital of Phoenicia, a narrow strip of land along the sea, west of Palestine. Here they found Christians and stayed with them for a week. It must have been rather wonderful to have been part of some little group of Christians in those days, mustn't it, and never know when Paul would drop in to stay with you?

Here also there were prophets who warned Paul not to go to Jerusalem, but he and his party went on just the same. All the Christians, even the children and babies, went to see Paul off. They all knelt down by the shore and prayed with him and said good-bye, and watched him board his ship before they went home.

The next port they touched at was Ptolemais, on the same coast as Tyre, just a little farther south. Here they stayed for one day with the Christians, and then went on to Caesarea.

Two old friends turn up again in this chapter. Do you remember Philip the deacon, who explained the Old Testament to Queen Candace's treasurer and converted him? Now this same Philip was living in Caesarea. He had four daughters who had the gift of prophecy, and Paul, Luke, and their party all stayed with him. People think that a lot of what Luke tells us about the Church in Jerusalem in its very first days was told to him by Philip.

And do you remember Agabus, the prophet who foretold the great famine? He came from Judea to see

The Riot in Ephesus

Paul at Caesarea. When he arrived he took the cord Paul wore around his waist to keep his clothes tidy and bound his own hands and feet with it, saying, "The Holy Spirit says that the man to whom this cord belongs will be bound like this by the Jews in Jerusalem and will be handed over to the Romans."

When they heard this everybody pleaded with Paul more than ever please to give up his plan of going to Jerusalem, just as Peter had pleaded with our Lord not to go there and die, but like our Lord, Paul knew he mustn't listen.

"What do you mean by going on like this and discouraging me?" he said. "For the name of the Lord Jesus, I am ready to meet prison and death, too, in Jerusalem."

So, as he would not listen, "We composed ourselves," Luke says, "and said, 'The Lord's will be done!' "

Chapter Eleven

Paul's Arrest in Jerusalem
(Acts 21 cont., 22, 23, 24, 25, 26)

They left Caesarea and set out for Jerusalem so as to arrive in good time for the feast of Pentecost. Some of the Christians from Caesarea joined the party; they wanted to bring Paul to the house of a man from Cyprus called Mnason who was one of the first converts there. He invited Paul and his companions to stay with him.

Of course, all the Christians in Jerusalem were delighted to see Paul. The day after they arrived the whole party went to see James, the bishop of Jerusalem, and found all the clergy of Jerusalem waiting with him to welcome them. Paul told them all that had been happening since he saw them last, and they thanked God with all their hearts for so much good news.

Then somebody said to Paul, "Brother, you will see for yourself that there are thousands of Jews in Jerusalem who have become good Christians, and they have all continued to follow the Jewish Law. Now, we have been hearing rumors that you tell the Jews in pagan countries that when they are converted they are to break away from the Law and to forget all their traditions. So what will happen? Why, as soon as they see

The First Christians

you, a crowd of them will pounce on you. Now, what we think you had better do is this. There are four poor men here who are under a vow; if you join with them in it and pay for them to have their heads shaved and their other expenses, then it will be clear to everyone that the reports they have heard about you are not true."

Paul thought this an excellent plan, as indeed it seemed to be, but it didn't turn out very well.

This vow that Paul made is the second one that we have heard about him making. He wasn't doing it only to impress the Jewish Christians by showing that he had not lost his respect for Jewish customs and the Jewish Law. What he and the four poor men whose expenses he was paying were to do was to shave their heads, go to the Temple every day for prayers, and offer a sacrifice there on the last day.

It all seems rather odd to us, doesn't it? But suppose that there was something you wanted very badly indeed. You might say, "I am going to make a really terrific novena to our Lady. I shall go to Mass every day, and make a visit in the afternoon, and I will give up candy for the nine days, and I shall ask Father So and So to say Mass for my intention on the ninth day, and I shall make an offering for the poor, too." You would have to want something badly, to do all that, wouldn't you? So would I! Or we might do as much to say a tremendous thank you for something we had prayed for and had been given.

Well, the idea of a vow was something like that. Paul and the four men spent most of their time in the Temple for the next week and all went well until the last day.

Paul's Arrest in Jerusalem

Then some of those Jews who had worried Paul in Ephesus arrived in Jerusalem and saw Paul there with one of his Gentile friends. People who were not Jews were forbidden under pain of death to go into the Temple, except just into the outer court, and when these same Jews saw Paul inside the Temple next day they jumped to the conclusion that he had brought his Gentile friend in with him. Or they pretended to. Anyway, they caught hold of Paul and shouted, "Men of Israel, help! Come to the rescue! Here is the man who goes about everywhere teaching people to despise us and our Law and this Temple — he has brought his Gentile friends into this holy place!"

There was an uproar: everyone set on Paul and dragged him out of the Temple and the priests inside slammed the gates to keep the crowd out. The Jews who had seized Paul beat him and would have killed him, but the captain of the Roman garrison heard what was happening in time and came to the rescue. He and his

soldiers charged into the mob, and when the crowd saw them, they stopped beating Paul.

That was a very quick rescue, wasn't it? But the soldiers lived in the Antonia, a fort that overlooked the Temple grounds, so it wouldn't have taken a moment for them to hear that there was trouble or to see where it was going on.

The captain, whose name was Lysias, arrested Paul, had him bound with a double chain and then asked if someone could tell him who he was and what he had done. But some people in the crowd shouted one thing and some another, and altogether there was so much noise and confusion he could make nothing of it, so he ordered the soldiers to take Paul to their quarters in the fortress.

When they reached the steps up to the fort, he had to be carried by the soldiers, because the crowd was pressing on them and shouting that he should be put to death forthwith.

Just as they reached the door to the soldiers' quarters, Paul turned to the captain and said, "May I speak to you a moment?"

"What?" said the captain. "Can you speak Greek? Why then, you can't be that Egyptian who raised an army of cut-throats some time ago and let them out into the desert?"

"I am a Jew," said Paul, rather crossly, I daresay, "a citizen of Tarsus in Cilicia, no mean city. What I want of you is a chance to speak to these people."

The captain said he might. So Paul stood up on the top of the steps and raised his hand for silence, and the whole crowd was suddenly quiet.

Paul's Arrest in Jerusalem

"Brethren and fathers," he began politely, and when they heard that he was speaking in their own language, they listened all the more attentively. "I am a Jew, born in Tarsus and brought up in this city, Jerusalem. I was taught to be as jealous of the honor of the Law as all you are today. I persecuted this Way," — Paul meant Christianity — "to the death, putting men and women in chains and sending them to prison.

"The chief priests will tell you this is true, for I went to Damascus with letters from them, meaning to take more prisoners there and bring them back to Jerusalem for punishment. But at midday, when I was already near to Damascus, a great light shone around me and I fell to the ground. I heard a voice say, 'Saul, Saul, why do you persecute me?' 'Who are you, Lord?' I asked, and He answered me, 'I am Jesus of Nazareth whom Saul persecutes.' My companions saw the light, but could not hear what was said to me. Then I said, 'What must I do, Lord?' and He said, 'Get up from the ground and go into Damascus and there you will be told what you are to do.'

"The glory of that light had blinded me and my companions had to lead me by the hand into the city. There a certain man called Ananias, well known to his Jewish neighbors for his care in following the Law, came and stood beside me and said, 'Brother Saul, look up and see!'

"And at once I looked up into his face and I could see again. Then he said, 'The God of our fathers has chosen you to know His will and to see the Just One (he meant our Lord) and to hear Him speak. What you have seen and heard you are to speak of to all men. Come on then, why are you wasting time? Get up and be baptized, washing away your sins and calling on His Name.'

"Afterwards, when I came back to Jerusalem again, I was praying in the Temple and I fell into a trance and saw the Lord there speaking to me. 'Make haste', He said, 'leave Jerusalem as fast as you can, they will not listen to you here.'

" 'Well, Lord,' I said, 'they know how I used to imprison those who believed in You and have them beaten in the synagogues, and when the blood of Stephen, Your martyr, was shed, I stood by approving of it and watching over the coats they had thrown off while they stoned him.'

"And He said, 'Go on your way, for I will send you to the pagans who live far away.' "

Until then the crowd had listened to Paul, but when he said that, they began to shout again because they couldn't bear the idea of God sending anyone to preach to people who were not Jews.

"Away with such a fellow!" they shouted. "It is a disgrace that he is allowed to live!" And they began to throw their coats and handfuls of dust in the air, and generally to be so noisy and hopeless that the captain had Paul taken inside, into the soldiers' quarters. He gave the soldiers orders to scourge Paul to make him say what he had done.

They had him tied up ready to be beaten when he said to them, "Have you any right to scourge a man who is a Roman citizen and who hasn't even been judged?"

The centurion who was in charge of Paul was startled. He went to Captain Lysias and said, "What are you thinking of? You told me to scourge this man and he is a

Paul's Arrest in Jerusalem

Roman citizen." This was a horrid shock to the captain; mistreating a Roman citizen was no joke. So he came to Paul and said, "What is this I hear? Are you really a Roman citizen?"

"Yes," said Paul.

"Why," said the captain, "it cost *me* plenty to become one."

"Ah," said Paul, "but I was born so." Which was rather a nice gentle snub, wasn't it?

After this the captain thought he had better be a bit more careful, so he took off Paul's bonds and said he would call a meeting of the Council for next morning and then Paul should have a proper chance to defend himself before the chief priests.

Next morning, just as he had said he would, the captain called the Jewish Council together and brought Paul before them. This captain wasn't going to have Paul ill-treated again, and besides he very much wanted to find out what all the fuss was about.

This is what Paul said to the Council, "Brethren, all my life I have been loyal in my conscience toward God." When the High Priest heard this he told the people standing near Paul to hit him on the mouth. "God will strike you," said Paul, "sitting there to judge me according to the Law and yourself disobeying the Law by telling people to hit me."

Somebody told him he was insulting the High Priest and Paul said he was sorry he couldn't see who it was from where he stood. But there was one thing he could see clearly enough and that was that he was not going to be allowed to make a proper speech defending himself. So he looked around and saw that there were both

The First Christians

Sadducees and Pharisees in the Council and he knew there was no love lost between them.

The two things they especially disagreed about were the resurrection of the dead and whether there were really any angels. The Pharisees believed in both, as we do, and as Paul did, but the Sadducees didn't believe in either.

So Paul thought he would come straight to the point both of Christian teaching and of their disagreement. He called out aloud, "I am a Pharisee and my fathers were Pharisees before me and I am on trial today because I believe in the resurrection of the dead."

This set the Council in a turmoil: the Sadducees were angrier than ever, but some of the Pharisees were no longer sure they were angry at all. Some of them stood up and came forward saying, "We have no fault to find with this man after all, perhaps an angel has spoken to him."

This enraged the Sadducees still more and there was such a row the captain was afraid Paul would be killed, so he sent his soldiers in to the Council to get Paul out and bring him safely back to the Antonia.

That night our Lord came and stood beside Paul and said to him, "Do not be discouraged. You are finished with witnessing for Me in Jerusalem, but you shall go to Rome and be my witness there."

In the morning some of the Jews met together and swore an oath that they would not eat or drink anything at all until they had killed Paul. There were more than forty of them who joined in this plot. They went to the chief priests and told them about it. "Your part in the business," they said, "is to persuade the captain to

Paul's Arrest in Jerusalem

send Paul to you, as if you meant to ask him some more questions, and when he is on his way, we will set upon him and kill him."

And so they would have done, if it had not been for a boy. He was Paul's nephew, his sister's son, and he heard what was said, and ran off to the Antonia and told his Uncle Paul about it.

Paul asked one of the soldiers to take his nephew to the captain. "He has some news for him," he said.

The captain took the boy by the hand and led him to one side. "What is it you have to tell me?" he said.

The boy (I wonder how old he was?) told the captain all about the plot to kill his uncle, and the captain told him to go home and not say a word about it to anyone else, and he would see to it.

So the boy ran off home, and that is all we know about him.

The captain still hadn't been able to make out why his own people were so angry with Paul, but he wasn't going to have a Roman citizen murdered while in his charge. So he gave orders to the officers under him that they were to set out that night to march to Caesarea with two hundred soldiers, two hundred spearmen and a troop of seventy cavalry soldiers and horses for Paul. They were to set out after dark and were to see Paul safe to the governor, Felix.

It was quite an escort, wasn't it? The captain was very determined to get Paul away safely. Luke says he was afraid that if the Jews killed Paul he would be accused of taking a bribe to give them the chance!

He sent a letter to Felix the governor. It is rather a nice letter, with just one small half-lie in it. See if you

The First Christians

can spot it: "Claudius Lysias sends greetings to His Excellency Felix the Governor. Here is a man whom the Jews seized and would have killed but I came up with my men and rescued him, understanding that he is a Roman citizen. I took him into the presence of their Council and tried to discover what they had against him, but I found it was all concerned with some dispute about their Law and that he was accused of nothing for which he ought to die or be punished. Now I have information of a plot they have made to kill him, so I am sending him to you and I shall tell his accusers that they must take the matter up with you."

Did you see the little half-lie? He says he rescued Paul because he "understood he was a Roman citizen," but that wasn't quite the way it happened, was it?

Well, this small army traveled all night with Paul but in the morning the foot soldiers halted and left the cavalry to escort Paul the rest of the way to Caesarea, and they arrived quite safely.

When the governor had read his letter from the captain in Jerusalem he told Paul he would hear his case when his accusers arrived from Jerusalem, and gave orders that in the meantime he was to be kept safely in Herod's Palace. There was no Herod living there now, it was where the governor himself lived.

Paul waited there five days and then the High Priest Ananias arrived in a very bad temper. With him were some of the other Jewish priests and a Roman lawyer called Tertullus, brought along especially to impress Felix the governor.

Felix sent for Paul and then sat down to judge the case.

Paul's Arrest in Jerusalem

Tertullus began his speech against Paul with very flowery compliments to Felix, all about how many wrongs he had set right and how peaceful everything had been while he had been governor. Then he came to the point. He said Paul was "a ringleader of the Nazarenes" and that he went about all over the world preaching to the Jews that they ought to revolt against the Romans and, he said, Paul violated the Temple — which made rather an odd mixture of things to bring against him.

"We arrested him," he went on, meaning the Jews had done so, "and meant to try him according to our Law, but Captain Lysias came and violently took him away and said his accusers must appear before you. Ask him some questions yourself, and you will soon see that all this is true."

The other Jews joined in and said that, yes, indeed this was all true, but the governor turned to Paul and made a sign that it was his turn to speak.

"I can defend myself all the more boldly," said Paul, "because I know you have been a judge over this country for many years. You can easily find out that I only came to Jerusalem twelve days ago to worship there. I have never been found making trouble in the Temple or in the synagogues or in the streets, and they can bring you no proof that I have.

"But I admit this much — that worshipping God, my Father, I follow what we call the Way and they call a sect. I put my trust in the Law and the prophets of the Jews, sharing with them the hope that all the dead will rise again, and I, like them, try to keep my conscience clean.

The First Christians

"After being away for some years, I came to Jerusalem bringing a gift of money for the men of my own race and offerings for the Temple. It was when I had just made these offerings that I was found there. There was no crowd about me, no sign of trouble, until some Jews from Asia suddenly set upon me. If those men have anything against me, why are they not here?

"Since they are not, let those Jews who have come say what they found out when I was examined by their Council. The only thing they have against me is this, that I cried out, 'If I am on trial today, it is because of the resurrection of the dead!'"

Felix, who knew a good deal about Christianity, and didn't think much of the charges against Paul, said he could not finish the case then. "I will hear you again," he said, "when Lysias comes down from Jerusalem." He wasn't expecting Lysias and as far as we know he never did come down, so I suppose the High Priest and the rest of the party went back to Jerusalem in no better temper than they had left it.

Felix gave orders that Paul was to be kept securely, but not made uncomfortable, and that any of his friends who came to visit him were to be allowed to see him.

So there was Paul, back in prison again, in the governor's palace, waiting to see what would happen next.

What did happen was that a few days later Felix and his wife, who was called Drusilla, sent for Paul because he and Drusilla wanted to hear more about our Lord.

I am sure you would never guess who Drusilla was. She was the great-granddaughter of the Herod who had all the babies in Bethlehem killed in the hope that one of them would be our Lord. Her father was the Herod

Paul's Arrest in Jerusalem

who killed James, the first Apostle to die, and who tried to kill Peter, too; and the Herod who made friends with Pontius Pilate over the trial of our Lord was her great uncle. They were a charming family, weren't they?

Drusilla was just the sort of girl you might expect. She was only nineteen when she came to Caesarea as Felix's wife, but she had been married already and had run away from her husband because she liked Felix better. I can't think why, because he doesn't seem to have been at all a pleasant sort of man.

Well, these two sent for Paul and asked him to tell them something about Christianity. So Paul, who, as you know, was never afraid of anybody, preached them a sermon on justice and purity and on the judgment we must all face when we die.

As Felix was anything but just, and he had just run away with somebody else's wife, he didn't care for this sermon at all, and I don't suppose Drusilla liked it any better. Felix was so frightened he said hastily that that would do for now. "I will send for you again some other day when I have more time," he said.

And in spite of being frightened, he did send for Paul several times and tried to make friends with him.

Can you guess why? He had heard that Paul brought money to Jerusalem for the poor there and that he had also brought an offering to the Temple, and he thought Paul must be quite rich and might perhaps like to offer him a bribe to be set free! And that, no doubt, is also why he wanted Paul to be as comfortable as possible in prison, and why all his friends were allowed to come and visit him — in case they were bringing money for a bribe.

The First Christians

Paul was in prison there for two years and then a new governor was appointed in place of Felix, but Felix left Paul still in prison because he thought it would please the Jews.

The new governor's name was Festus and he was a much better sort of man than Felix.

Three days after he arrived in Palestine, Festus went up to Jerusalem to see how things were going there. Of course the High Priest and the other leading Jews came to him and told him their story of what an awful sort of man Paul was. They asked him to send for Paul so that his case could be tried in Jerusalem, but what they meant to do was to lie in ambush on the way and kill Paul before he arrived.

But Festus, luckily, would not agree. "Nonsense," he said, "he is quite safe in Caesarea and I shall be going there myself in a few days. If any of you have something against him, you can travel down with me and I will hear the case when I arrive."

So they had to be content with that.

The morning after the new governor, and all the people with him, including these Jews, arrived, Paul was brought to the judgment hall.

The Jews accused him of all sorts of crimes, which, Luke says mildly, "They could not prove."

Then Paul spoke in his own defense, "I have committed no crime against the Jewish Law or against the Temple, or against Caesar," he said.

Festus, who of course didn't know all that had been going on before he arrived, said to Paul, "Are you willing to go up to Jerusalem and there meet these charges before me?"

Paul's Arrest in Jerusalem

"No," said Paul, "I am standing now at Caesar's judgment seat, where I ought to be judged. As for the Jews, I have done them no wrong, as you very well know. If I am guilty and deserve death, I do not ask to be let off, but if their charges are false, no one has a right to make them a present of my life." And then he said the words that any Roman citizen might say if he was not satisfied with the way his case was being tried, "I appeal to Caesar."

This surprised Festus, and he went aside for a moment to talk it over with the people who advised him. Then he came back and said to Paul, "So you appeal to Caesar? Very well, to Caesar you shall go."

That was one way to get to Rome, wasn't it?

Paul had to wait some time until there would be a boat going that could take him there. While he was waiting, visitors arrived to stay with Festus.

You remember Drusilla, Felix's wife, who was the great-granddaughter of Herod who killed all the babies in Bethlehem? Well, these visitors were her brother, King Herod Agrippa II, and her sister Bernice.

Agrippa was allowed the title of king by the Romans, but you aren't really much of a king if the real rulers of your country say whether you can be called so or not. So these two were coming, very politely, to pay their respects to Festus (who was living in their family's palace, by the way).

Festus thought it would be a good idea to discuss Paul's case with them: perhaps they would understand what was really the trouble between Paul and the Jews of Jerusalem better than he did. So he said to Agrippa, "There is a man here whom Felix left behind in prison.

The First Christians

The Jews wanted me to condemn him to death, but I told them that it is not the Roman custom to pronounce sentence until the man accused has had a chance to clear himself. So they came here with me and I did not keep them waiting — the very next day I sat in the judgment seat and had this man brought in.

"But his accusers seemed to have no real crime to charge him with, only some silly business of their own and something to do with a dead man called Jesus, who Paul said was alive. I did not want to meddle with such matters, so I asked Paul if he were willing to go to Jerusalem to be judged there. But he appealed to Caesar and is now waiting here until I can send him to Rome."

"I have heard about this man," said Agrippa, "and as a matter of fact, I have often wanted to hear him speak."

"Right," said Festus. "You shall hear him tomorrow."

The next day Festus made a very grand party for his visitors. Agrippa and Bernice came into the great hall in their grandest clothes and all the important people who lived in Caesarea came, too, and it was all quite glittering and exciting.

Festus had Paul brought in and then stood up and made a speech. "King Agrippa," he said, "and all you who are here today: you see before you a man whom all the Jews want me to put to death — they say he ought not to be allowed to live a day longer. For myself, I am certain he has done nothing that deserves death, but he has appealed to Caesar, so I must send him to Rome.

"Now my difficulty is this. I am supposed to send a letter with him saying what he is charged with, and I can discover nothing to say. So I have brought him

Paul's Arrest in Jerusalem

before you all, and especially you, King Agrippa, hoping that you may help me to find something to write to Caesar. It seems to me quite unreasonable to send a prisoner to Rome and not say what he is charged with." Then Festus sat down and signed to Agrippa to take over.

"You are now free to give an account of yourself," Agrippa said to Paul.

"King Agrippa," said Paul, "I count myself lucky to be defending myself against the Jews' accusations before you. I know that you know all about Jewish customs and what questions they argue about, so I feel sure you will listen to me patiently. All the Jews know (if they would just admit it) that I have lived from my childhood a Pharisee. If I am on trial today it is for the hope of the promise God made to our fathers — it is for this hope, my lord king, that they accuse me. Why can't they believe that God can bring the dead to life again?"

Then he went on to tell them how he used to persecute the Christians and of his vision of our Lord on the way to Damascus, and how from then on he had been sent to preach about Him to the pagans far away.

"That," he said, "is why the Jews tried to murder me in the Temple. There is nothing in my preaching that goes beyond what the prophets spoke of as things to come: they told us to expect a suffering Christ and one who would give light to His own people and to the pagans by being the first to rise from the dead."

When he had gone so far, Festus, to whom this talk of rising from the dead seemed pure nonsense, cried out in a loud voice, "Paul, you are mad! You have studied too long and it has affected your mind!"

The First Christians

Paul answered, "No, most noble Festus, I am not mad. What I say is plain truth. The king knows all about it, that is why I speak with confidence in his presence. This is no news to him, the things that have been happening were not done in some corner." Then he turned to Agrippa again and said, "Do you believe the prophets, King Agrippa? I know you do."

"You would like to make a Christian of me very easily," said King Agrippa.

"I wish I could," said Paul, "whether easily or not — I wish everyone here today was just as I am, except for these chains."

But Agrippa did not want to hear any more, so he got up, to show he was finished. Paul was taken back to his prison, and the party went on.

Afterward the guests said to one another, "This man is not guilty of anything that deserves imprisonment or death."

And Agrippa said to Festus, "He might have been set free, if he had not appealed to Caesar."

Chapter Twelve

Paul Goes to Rome
(Acts 27, 28)

Paul had been waiting some time longer in the governor's palace at Caesarea when word came that there was at last a ship sailing on which he and the other prisoners who were being sent to Rome could begin their journey.

It was high time they were off because it was already August and sailing in the Mediterranean in the Fall could be very dangerous in those days. There were no compasses to help sailors find their way; they had to judge where they were by the position of the sun by day and the stars by night, and when you think how often you can't see the sun or the stars for clouds or fog, you won't wonder that ships used to stay in sight of land as much as they could.

Still, the voyage to Rome would only take about ten days with luck, so they thought there was plenty of time to get there before stormy Fall weather began.

There was a company of Roman soldiers in charge of the prisoners going to Rome, and the officer in charge was called Julius. Luke and Aristarchus, a friend of Paul's from Thessalonica, went along on the same

The First Christians

boat as passengers. They meant to look after Paul on the journey and keep him company, and to see what happened when he got to Rome.

The ship sailed north up the coast from Caesarea and the next day came to Sidon. There were Christians there, and Julius, the centurion, was very nice to Paul — he let him go and visit them. From there they sailed on, keeping under the lee of the island of Cyprus as long as they could because the wind was against them, but they managed to cross the open sea to a port called Myra on the south coast of Turkey.

This was as far as that ship was going, so the centurion had to look around for one that would take them on to Italy. He soon found one, a big ship, carrying wheat and passengers from Alexandria, and Paul and all the rest of the party went on board her.

They sailed as far as Gnidus, a port on the cape at the southwest tip of Turkey, going very slowly, and with great difficulty, for the winds were still against them the whole time.

After they left Gnidus it was even worse: they crept along under the lee of Crete, and at last managed to reach a harbor called Fair Havens on the south coast of that island. They had wasted so much time by then because of the winds beating the ship back that it was already late in September and sailing was becoming more dangerous every day.

Paul told them to make the best of Fair Havens, although it wasn't a very good harbor for a big ship to winter in. "Sirs," he said, "I can see that if you try to go farther now, the ship will be in danger, and so shall we. We had much better stay where we are."

Paul Goes to Rome

Paul had been on so many voyages that his advice was well worth listening to, but the captain of the ship didn't agree with him, and the centurion thought the captain probably knew best, so it was decided to sail on along the coast of Crete to another harbor, only about thirty miles away, which was much better protected. So, on a lovely day with a gentle breeze blowing from the south, they set out. And all at once they found they had better have listened to Paul. A terrible storm came up with a great wind blowing from the northeast. It was so sudden and strong they could only let it take the ship where it pleased and they were soon blown quite off their course.

They were driven under the lee of an island called Cauda, about twenty miles south of Crete, where the wind was a little less violent, and they managed to pull the ship's boat on board, everybody helping. This boat was towed behind the ship in ordinary weather and was used for taking people ashore, bringing supplies on board and so on.

After that, they attended to making everything about the ship as safe as they could. The storm had come up so suddenly there had been no chance to do so before.

Then, because they were afraid of being driven on the quicksands of the shore to the south of them, they put out what Luke calls a sea anchor. It was a heavy plank of wood that trailed after them in the sea and slowed the ship down a little.

After that there was no more to do but drift with the storm, and hope it might soon blow over, but it did nothing of the kind; it kept on getting worse.

The First Christians

Next day the waves were so wild that the sailors lightened the ship by throwing some of the cargo overboard, and the day after that they even threw out some of the ship's gear. For days and days the storm went on, until no one had the least idea where they were, and no one dared hope ever to see land again. They were so desperate they didn't even bother to eat.

But at last Paul stood up among them and said, "Sirs, you should have listened to me and stayed in Fair Havens," — as if they doubted that now — "then you would have been spared all this loss and damage. But never mind, cheer up — none of you are going to be drowned. The ship will be lost, but that's all. Last night the God I serve sent an angel to me. He told me to have no fear, that I should stand in Caesar's presence at last and that God had granted me that all of us should be saved from the sea.

"Have courage then. I trust in God that all will happen as He told me. The next thing you know, we shall be cast up on an island."

Sure enough, fourteen nights after the storm began, the sailors began to think that there was land near them. They took soundings and found the sea was only twenty fathoms deep, and then took them again a little farther on and found it was only fifteen fathoms. So, for fear of being driven onto a rocky coast they put out four anchors from the stern and waited for daylight.

But the sailors thought they would let the ship's boat down and get away by themselves before daybreak: they pretended they were going to put down more anchors. But Paul saw what they were up to in time and told the centurion and his soldiers.

Paul Goes to Rome

"If the sailors leave us," he said, "there is no chance of safety." So the soldiers cut the ropes that held the boat and let it fall into the sea.

Then Paul looked around at all the wet and miserable people about him and made a very sensible suggestion. "This is the fourteenth day," he said, "that we have had no proper meal. What we need is a good breakfast. Come along now, it will help you to have something to eat. None of you are going to be drowned, or to be any the worse for what has happened." Then he took up a loaf of bread, broke a piece off and began to eat it.

When the other people in the ship saw him so cheerful they began to cheer up a little themselves and were quite willing to eat a meal. Afterward, I have no doubt, things looked brighter. They generally do after breakfast.

It was still dark, but they thought it would help them to run the ship ashore more safely when day came if it were not so heavy. So they threw the rest of their cargo of wheat into the sea.

When daylight came at last they saw that the coast they were close to was strange to them, not, as they had hoped, some place they could recognize from other voyages. But there was a sloping shore at one place that looked like a good spot to run the ship onto, so they pulled up the anchors and made for it. The front part of the ship struck into the sand and held fast, but the stern was all the more at the mercy of the waves and began to break up.

The soldiers thought that now they should kill the prisoners in case any of them swam ashore and escaped.

The First Christians

That sounds very cruel, but the soldiers knew that if any of the prisoners escaped the soldiers themselves would be killed for having lost them.

The centurion wouldn't allow it though: he liked Paul too much to let him be killed. Instead, he said that everyone who could swim was to go overboard first and help the rest to reach the land on planks and floating wreckage from the ship.

It must have been very frightening and very exciting, but one way and another they all did get safely out of the sea, just as Paul had told them they would.

Do you know where they were? On the island of Malta. They had been wrecked on its north coast: if it had been the south coast, where boats usually went, some one would certainly have recognized it.

You can see Malta on the map, down below Sicily. If you find Crete, too, you will see what a long way the ship had been driven by the storm.

The people who lived in that part of Malta had seen the shipwreck and came down to the shore to see if anyone had got safely ashore.

Paul Goes to Rome

Luke says they were very kind to the poor wet people off the ship and welcomed them by lighting a big fire to warm them. It was beginning to rain and it was chilly.

Paul collected a bundle of sticks to put on the fire and picked up a viper, which is a little poisonous snake, among them, without noticing it. As he was putting them on the fire the viper woke up and bit him.

When the people of Malta saw that they said to each other, "This man must be a murderer, he has escaped from the sea, but divine vengeance has seen to it that he will die all the same." They knew very well that a viper's bite is deadly.

Paul wasn't at all concerned — he knew that God wanted him to get safely to Rome — so he just shook the viper off and went on as usual. The people of Malta kept watching him, expecting him to fall down dead. When they saw that nothing happened and he seemed perfectly well and cheerful they changed their minds about him being a murderer and decided he must be a god.

The Roman in charge of Malta, the most important man on the island, was called Publius. He had large estates near where the ship was wrecked and when he heard about it, he said that all the people from the ship were to stay with him for a few days, until they had recovered and could find places to lodge until they could go on again.

Not everybody would have been so kind to a crowd of wet and hungry strangers, but Publius was well rewarded. His father was very ill with dysentery and fever and Paul cured him.

The First Christians

When news of this got about, every sick person on the island was brought to Paul, and he cured every one of them. No wonder that when they were able to leave Malta, Paul and his companions were loaded with gifts!

No one was going to try any more sailing in the Fall after the adventures they had had, so they all settled down on Malta for the winter.

About three months later it was all right to start out and they all got on board another wheat ship that had spent the winter in the harbor there.

They sailed first to Syracuse in Sicily, from there to Rhegium, on the toe of Italy's boot, and then on up the coast of Italy to Puteoli, which is in the bay of Naples, and that was as far as the ship was going.

Here there were Christians and they persuaded Paul, and Julius, the centurion who was in charge of the prisoners, to stay with them for a week. I think Julius was so fond of Paul by this time he would have done anything to please him.

While they were there one of the Christians of Puteoli must have gone on ahead to Rome, one hundred and forty miles away, to tell the Christians there that Paul was on his way to them, because some of them came as much as fifty miles to meet him. They met at a place called the Three Taverns, and ten miles farther on there even were more people waiting for him. It cheered Paul up very much that they should welcome him like this, and he thanked God for it.

When at last they all arrived in Rome, Paul was allowed to choose his own lodging and to live there while he was waiting for his case to be heard. He had to have a soldier living there too, who was supposed to

Paul Goes to Rome

guard him, and whenever he went out the soldier had to go, too, with his left wrist chained to Paul's right wrist. But this was much better than being in prison, and if Julius had anything to do with it, I am sure only the friendliest and nicest soldiers were allowed the duty of guarding Paul.

Three days after he arrived, Paul called a meeting of the leading men among the Jews of Rome. The Jews had all been sent away from Rome some time before, if you remember, but evidently they had been allowed to come back by now.

When they arrived, Paul made them a speech, and this is what he said, "I have done nothing against our people or our customs, yet the Jews in Jerusalem handed me over to the Romans as a prisoner. The Romans could find nothing against me and would have set me free, but the Jews still insisted I ought to be killed. That is why I appealed to Caesar. I have asked you to come here so that I could explain to you that it is only because I hope as you do that I wear this chain."

He meant it was because he hoped in the resurrection of the dead, as he had told the Jews in Jerusalem.

The Jews of Rome answered that no message about him had been sent to them and that they would very much like to hear what he had to say — all they had heard about the Christians, they said, was that they were hated everywhere.

So after that they arranged to spend a whole day with Paul and to hear all about the kingdom of God. When they came he did his best to show them from the writings of the prophets that our Lord was the Savior they had expected so long.

The First Christians

Some of them were convinced, but others could not believe it, and they all went home at last, still arguing.

After this Paul said, "The Holy Spirit did indeed tell the truth when he said to our fathers through the prophet Isaiah, 'Go to this people and tell them: "You will listen and listen, but you will not understand; you will look and look but you will not see the truth. The heart of this people has become dull. Their ears are slow to hear and they shut their eyes in case they should see: they will not come back to me and win healing from me." ' I give you notice then, that this message of salvation has been sent by God to the pagans, and they at least will listen to it."

For two whole years Paul lived in his lodgings in Rome, with a soldier to guard him, but otherwise free. He was waiting all that time for his case to come up. He could have as many visitors as he pleased and could preach, too, and no one interfered with him.

With him, we may suppose, lived Luke, busily writing his second book, the Acts of the Apostles. We have come to the end of it now.

Luke never tells us that Paul was at last tried and released, but he must have been, because we know that Paul went on still more journeys afterward and at last came back to Rome and had his head cut off by Nero, who also killed Peter.

Why do you suppose Luke doesn't tell us any of those things? The best guess anyone can make is that they hadn't happened yet.

Luke's book was written to tell about the first beginnings of the Church and how it spread into the world. So Luke just tells us the first part of Peter's story, the

Paul Goes to Rome

story of the very first Christians, and the story of Paul's preaching all over the world before he first came to Rome because these were the parts that he knew best.

Like Luke, I have left out a lot that I might have told you: it seemed to me that if I didn't stick fairly closely to what Luke said in Acts, we should never come to an end. So, like him, I have said nothing about all the letters Paul wrote, or about what we know from those letters of still other adventures that he had.

After all, every author has to leave something out, even Luke and I. But if you want to know more about Peter and Paul you can find — at the end of your New Testament — the letters that each of them wrote, and someday I hope you will have a chance to go to Jerusalem to see where the Church began, and to Rome to see where Peter and Paul went and where they died and are still so well remembered.

Biographical Note

Marigold Hunt
(1905-1994)

Marigold Hunt was a speaker for the Catholic Evidence Guild and served for many years as advertising manager of Sheed and Ward publishing company. In addition to this book, she wrote *St. Patrick's Summer, A Book of Angels,* and *A Life of Our Lord for Children*. Miss Hunt spent her final years in Somerset, Massachusetts, with her friends Patricia and Owen McGowan. She died on December 15, 1994, and is buried in St. Patrick's Cemetery in Somerset.

Sophia Institute

Sophia Institute is a nonprofit institution that seeks to nurture the spiritual, moral, and cultural life of souls and to spread the Gospel of Christ in conformity with the authentic teachings of the Roman Catholic Church.

Sophia Institute Press fulfills this mission by offering translations, reprints, and new publications that afford readers a rich source of the enduring wisdom of mankind.

Sophia Institute also operates two popular online Catholic resources: CrisisMagazine.com and CatholicExchange.com.

Crisis Magazine provides insightful cultural analysis that arms readers with the arguments necessary for navigating the ideological and theological minefields of the day. *Catholic Exchange* provides world news from a Catholic perspective as well as daily devotionals and articles that will help you to grow in holiness and live a life consistent with the teachings of the Church.

In 2013, Sophia Institute launched Sophia Institute for Teachers to renew and rebuild Catholic culture through service to Catholic education. With the goal of nurturing the spiritual, moral, and cultural life of souls, and an abiding respect for the role and work of teachers, we strive to provide materials and programs that are at once enlightening to the mind and ennobling to the heart; faithful and complete, as well as useful and practical.

Sophia Institute gratefully recognizes the Solidarity Association for preserving and encouraging the growth of our apostolate over the course of many years. Without their generous and timely support, this book would not be in your hands.

www.SophiaInstitute.com
www.CatholicExchange.com
www.CrisisMagazine.com
www.SophiaInstituteforTeachers.org

Sophia Institute Press® is a registered trademark of Sophia Institute. Sophia Institute is a tax-exempt institution as defined by the Internal Revenue Code, Section 501(c)(3). Tax I.D. 22-2548708.

Printed by Libri Plureos GmbH in Hamburg, Germany